MOVING PICTURES

Their Impact on Society

A facsimile reprint collection

JEROME S. OZER Publisher
1971

Advisory Editor: GARTH S. JOWETT

Library of Congress Catalog Card No. 78-160245

Manufactured in the United States of America

The Movies on Trial

THE VIEWS AND OPINIONS OF OUTSTANDING PERSONALITIES ANENT SCREEN ENTERTAINMENT PAST AND PRESENT

Compiled and Edited

by

WILLIAM J. PERLMAN

NEW YORK

THE MACMILLAN COMPANY

1936

PRINTED IN THE UNITED STATES-OF AMERICA
NORWOOD PRESS LINOTYPE, INC.
NORWOOD, MASS., U.S.A.

CONTENTS

vi   *Contents*

INTRODUCTION

WHY THIS BOOK?

A LITTLE over a year ago a storm of protest swept across the country against the kind of movies the motion picture industry had been offering for public entertainment. Civic and religious leaders, alarmed by the films' exploitation of indecency, exhorted a movie-going public to withhold its patronage from picture houses until the screen had been made safe for the "family." From the pulpit, from the rostrum, from the floors of legislation chambers, accusers pointed menacing fingers at Hollywood. A bill for national censorship of the movies was introduced in Congress. States and municipalities proposed fanatical laws which would have barred ninety per cent of the moving pictures produced. Clubs and organizations of various complexions and denominations pledged themselves to stay away from picture theatres. The general economic upheaval had already somewhat depleted the attendance of movie theatres, and a boycott, now imminent, threatened to cut down the attendance still more. Truly, the motion picture industry faced the greatest crisis since its inception.

Whether all the censure heaped upon the movies was justified is a moot question. We are of the opinion that it was not—at least on the grounds generally advanced. But, as in the case of most reform movements, the pendulum had been allowed to swing too far in one direction. Similar attacks have been launched, from time to time, against the stage, books, paintings, sculpture, and other artistic expressions. The trouble with the movies is not that they are indecent but that they are generally vapid and inane. If the screen had offered entertainment not quite so asinine, the agitation against it would have never gained impetus, all the charges of immorality notwithstanding. However, it must be admitted that the agitation, regardless of its justification, has achieved beneficial results. There have already come out of Hollywood pictures that have some sense to them. "One Night of Love," "Richelieu," "Les Misérables," "Ruggles of Red Gap," just to name a few at random, are a credit to the industry. The question is, how long will this good work be kept up?

Now that public indignation against the movies has subsided, an attempt has been made to present, between the covers of this volume, the issues involved in the recent controversy. With no intention other than to obtain a crystallized view of the various currents of opinion, outstanding personalities of the stage, screen, pulpit, press, bench, and classroom have been invited to participate in the discussion.

The influence of the screen for good or evil cannot be overestimated. As a propaganda medium it is the most powerful of agents. Napoleon said he feared one newspaper more than a thousand bayonets. What would he have said had he lived in the age of the cinema? Prob-

ably, that he feared one newsreel more than an army
corps. Upton Sinclair admits that it was movie-propa-
ganda that cost him the Governorship of California.
The business of making movies can no longer be considered the private concern of a few individuals. It may
be their private property but not their private concern—
not with seventy million patrons visiting the movies
weekly. The business is, potentially, too dangerous a
weapon to be entrusted to any group of individuals
without some sort of supervision. By supervision we do
not mean to suggest legal censorship; but the powers-
that-be of the industry should heed the wishes of the
intelligent minority, now and then, and not always try
to cater to the tastes of morons.

The studio executives whom we invited to join the
symposium referred us to the Association of Motion
Picture Producers (a subsidiary of the Motion Picture
Producers and Distributors of America, Inc., whose president is Will H. Hays, former Postmaster General of the
United States). The Producers' Association viewed our
project with suspicion and distrust. After weeks of ne-
gotiations and conferences, the matter was referred back
to the studios. After further discussion, four of the major
studios consented to contribute articles by important
executives. However, these had not been received when
the date of delivery of the manuscript to the publishers
approached; and requests to the studios for a definite
promise of delivery of the articles brought a final refusal
to be represented in a book thought to contain "much
material . . . that is derogatory to the motion picture
industry."

The vacillation and indisposition of the industry as a whole to meet the issue in respect to this book do not warrant the belief that Hollywood has suddenly reformed.

The accusation that we have gone out of our way to defame the movies will, of course, become pointless to any one reading this volume. Some of the chapters are not only not condemnatory but most commendatory. The articles of Judge Ben B. Lindsey and Judge Jonah J. Goldstein, two gentlemen who, by virtue of their experience with juvenile delinquents, are eminently fit to discuss the screen's influence on the adolescent, are really briefs for the movies. Both ridicule the idea advanced by reformers that some of the moving pictures with their unsavory topics have had a malevolent influence upon the youth. On the contrary, both contend that the movies have really benefited our youth morally and otherwise because they serve to keep them out of the streets and bad associations.

Other articles, notably by Gabriela Mistral, the Spanish poetess, Edward G. Robinson, Dr. Phelps and Brock Pemberton, equally commend the movies, for one reason or another, as an indispensable form of entertainment for the masses. There are other contributors whose quarrel with the movies is from purely an artistic and technical angle, giving credit and blame where they are due. Moreover, it is noteworthy that almost without exception the contributors are unanimously opposed to any form of censorship of the screen. If several take the movies to task for their portrayal of indecencies and their sinister influence upon the youth's morale, we must be tolerant

of their views as we are of those who are more favorably
disposed toward this ever recurrent question of morals.

THE EDITOR.

HOLLYWOOD, CALIFORNIA
  June 1, 1935

NOTE: Grateful acknowledgement is hereby made to the
Editor of the *Delineator* for permission to include in this volume
Dr. Phelps' article; to the Ecclesiastical Review for permission to
reprint the chapter by the Most Reverend John J. Cantwell, D.D.;
"The Motion Picture Industry"; to William Allen White and to
Upton Sinclair for *their* chapters.

THE MOVIES ON TRIAL

CHAPTER I

CHEWING-GUM RELAXATION

by

WILLIAM ALLEN WHITE

SOME years back, before the advent of the talkies, I said some things about the movies which were not at all complimentary to their makers. I regret to say that the billions of feet of celluloid that have come out of Hollywood since do not warrant a change of my views. What effect the recent agitation against the movies will have on screen entertainment remains to be seen. I can only judge them by their past performances.

Every one agrees that the moving picture either is a mess or a menace, unless he is one of two classes: those who regularly go to the movies and those who make them.

There are millions who do not go to moving pictures but who would go if they could. No one is making pictures for them.

Speaking rather broadly, and allowing for some exceptions, the outcasts from the moving-picture world are the intelligent people. They have no time for the movies because the movies generally have no time for intelligent people.

That also is subject to some amendment and to considerable debate. For it must be conceded that from half

3

a dozen to a score of the motion pictures offered every year should interest intelligent people. But that is an infinitesimally small number of pictures compared with the output of the film makers.

Perhaps the leadership of America—the minority with critical intelligence—does not deserve the consideration of the men who are making fabulous fortunes out of the movies by appealing to the uncritical group. Put upon a financial basis—the basis of their potential patronage in dollars—the claims of the minority that avoids the movies are not valid. Put upon any other basis, their demands are righteous. For until the moving picture accepts the dictum and the leadership of the critically intelligent minority the industry will continue to be the dumb, flashy sister among the muses that she is; the sister of easy money and easy morals.

The trouble with the moving-picture business is chiefly the lack of standards graded by intelligence. Now, the word intelligence must be defined for the use of this article. The word refers to the minority with an aesthetic sense, with some feeling for the meaning of what is called art: either a feeling instinctive or consciously cultivated for the business of conveying ideas and emotions which we call good taste. Certainly the feeling is not prudery nor pruriency nor any related thing. The feeling is shocked by banality as deeply as by license. So we may say that intelligence in watching moving pictures is manifested by one who has a broad intellectual tolerance, restricted by a moral gumption which rejects stupidity in any of its gaudy forms.

The intelligent group in any community demands

grades in all forms of artistic expression, for sheer convenience. Chromos, jazz, Rogers groups, Uncle Tom's Cabins, Ouidas, all have their rights, their place in a wide cosmos, but intelligence has no time for these. So with moving pictures. They also must be graded or altogether avoided.

The standards that exist are worthless. They are set too frequently only by the money spent on a production—money spent for actors, for scenic effects, for various material accessories. The money spent for ideas rarely enters the gauge in grading a picture. It is billed as "magnificent," "gorgeous," "thrilling," "gripping," but never as profound, baffling, delightful, whimsical or stimulating. When a new movie is exhibited—and many are exhibited in the course of a year—that is marked by any sort of artistic appeal, if nothing else can bait the hook for the slow-witted, the name of the actor in the movie is blazoned upon the boards. For a picture is at the mercy of its stupidest patrons.

The best books, the best plays, the best music and the best poetry are written frankly for the discerning and the wise. The best in all other arts is conceived, produced, sold and lives or dies solely and with brutal frankness for the approval of the intelligent: in all the arts except in the movies. There, no artists, no directors, no writers, no theatres and no producers are set apart to please people of understanding. The Scarlet Muse of the silver screen sees only money, big money, quick money, the dirty money of her dupes.

Vapid and indecent books, paintings, sculptures, music

and plays are offered to the public as well as banal or erotic movies. But the point lies here: the men and women who do trite and dirty things with words and lines and sounds have small fame and little standing for all their huge profits; while, because of their huge financial takings, and often for no other reason, many cheap and shameless figures have standing in the movie world; indeed, are often the people best known by the multitude. Hollywood beckons daily to its portals any number of fine creative artists, but their stay there is generally of short duration. For they soon discover that the producers do not want their art; they only wish to use their names, as an advertising medium.

And of what use can the creative artist really be to the movies? Creative genius of a high order generally appeals first to the intelligent, then to the unintelligent who accept the leadership of those who can tell the good from the bad. But in all the movie world no place is provided where persons of wit or gumption may go to find screen entertainment that is directed at the discriminating.

If, in America, Booth Tarkington, Sherwood Anderson, Edna St. Vincent Millay, Sinclair Lewis, Willa Cather and Robert Frost had access to no other public except that which reads True Stories, Snappy Stories or Adventures, or only to publications that appeal to vacant minds; if George Bellows, Douglas Volk, Gutzon Borglum, or John Sargent had been dependent on minds that are satisfied with the comic strips, where would the creative intelligence, interpreting life in terms of truth, find an encouraging public or a living wage?

Now and again—perhaps a dozen times a year—something is produced on the screen which gladdens the understanding heart. But in the flood of chaff the wheat is lost. The shallow, the sappy, the spoony, the heavy and the blatant cover the good seed. It is not graded, therefore it creates no standard.

And there is the crux of the whole matter—the ordinary moving-picture circuit. The moving-picture business should be graded and classified by houses, as, for instance, the theatre was graded before the moving-picture business came to destroy the provincial stage.

The situation that confronts intelligent people in America in relation to the moving-picture business is exactly that which would be created if the New Jersey publisher of pornographic vapidity and the Chicago publisher of Wild and Woolly stories should buy up the Atlantic Monthly, The New Republic, Scribner's, Collier's, The American Mercury and their kindred contemporaries, and pour the intellectual dishwater and incidental slops of the New Jersey and Chicago publications into the older literary receptacles; while betimes poking in something from H. L. Mencken, Edgar Lee Masters, Dorothy Canfield Fisher, Edith Wharton and Carl Sandburg, to make a septic swill!

To clarify this, let us put it another way. Two or three years ago a strong American story sold a quarter of a million copies in book form and was palpably a financial success. The story attracted the motion-picture producers. They bought the movie rights to it. The story dramatized an idea; the idea being that life has other values than material ones, that America needs beauty more than it needs wealth, and that it profiteth a man nothing to gain the whole world and lose his soul. That was the story. And a studio paid the author a king's ransom for the right to reproduce the story on the screen.

But the studio did not use the story. It could not use it. To tell that story to a crowd of loose-jawed morons sitting in the average movie theatre would, first, make them blink; second, make them yawn; and third, move them out of the theatre in wild amazement.

So the motion-picture magnate paid, say, fifty or seventy-five thousand dollars for what? For two words: the title. They reasoned well that their customers had heard of the book; that they were possibly incapable of reading it, and that they would like to talk as if they knew about the book. So they took the title and, saving the names but not in the least the spirit of some of the characters, made another story of it, smeared it with a mush of sex and excitement and purveyed it to their patrons in the form which their patrons required! On the other hand, Tolstoy's, "Resurrection," an author and a book known to every intelligent person, was put on the screen under the name of "We Live Again."

Why do they do this? Because, in the first instance, the movie producers have developed no market in the moving-picture business for the kind of story the American author wrote. In the case of Tolstoy's novel, I suppose the producer feared that the vast majority of the movie-going public would not know the meaning of "Resurrection," so he defined the meaning of the word for his patrons.

The gulf is abysmal between the moving-picture audience and the *particular* movie-going audience which would have been attracted to a story with an intelligent appeal regardless of the name attached to it.

What the motion-picture industry must have, before it becomes anything but a by-word, is a string of theatres across the land that will advertise, "Lowbrows, Cripple-wits and Sex-seekers barred from this house."

Given ten or twenty million dollars—no large sum when one considers what it would achieve in American life—a theatre would be chartered in every country town of more than twenty-five thousand inhabitants where the minority that loves truth in art could find it in the movie.

That does not mean "clean, wholesome plays"—nothing like it. That means, rather, a selective reality in the presentation of life that makes truth rise and shine in a picture. It does not mean salacious plays—quite the contrary. It means sex would not be snubbed or repressed, but also neither emphasized nor exploited, but take its place candidly as a part of life and its motives.

This all means that the motion-picture industry might develop an art, as writing and painting and sculpture and the drama have developed arts, without the accursed censorship of the aesthetically lame and the halt and the blind forever snuffing out the fire of truth in the movie as ignorance puts out the divine fire. In recent years the movies have relied upon the gangster and the harlot for entertainment of the public. Fancy a movie with a dubious but struggling hero, a good but incompetent villain, perverse innocence and humor that gets nothing gayer than a smile.

In every unit of twenty thousand people, congregated

as an American town or neighborhood, two or three movie theatres thrive. Why not segregate the highbrows in one house—the smallest? They could be taught to fill it every night.

Now, the answer to this thesis, of course, will come back from the makers of the movies that the intelligent public, does not care for intelligent movies. The movie makers contend that theirs is not essentially a medium for conveying information or controversial ideas but is merely a means for occupying somewhat the same place in the schedule of an intelligent person as detective stories occupy in literature; something to amuse, to divert, to pass an idle hour. The movie makers, in substantiating their claim that the motion picture is not a medium intended to convey serious ideas, will cite the classic modern instance: In a Western state a state federation of women's clubs had met to denounce bad moving pictures. But the members of the federation went *en masse* to a bad picture and neglected a good one which the thoughtful exhibitors of the town had provided for the session of the federation.

Of course the episode is true, but it proves nothing except that the women had been fooled so many times by high talk of "clean, wholesome movies," which were merely stupid and badly done, that they took a chance to see a well-known lady with a marathon kiss, which they knew would be as advertised.

Criticism of the motion-picture industry comes down to this: The business is not intellectually honest because it is not intellectual. It has no notion of how bad it is because it has developed no commanding artist who has power to follow his intelligent instincts and to develop an intelligent public. An artist can express himself freely in literature, in painting, in music, in sculpture, because the cost of production and distribution of the fine arts is low. So your genuine artist can find his public, can even make it, can hold it, can enlarge it. But the cost of production and distribution in the movie business is so high that the dollar dominates the art and controls its forms—not the artist. Hence the moving-picture output is controlled by business sense. The rules of the motion-picture business are based on business sense, not on artistic sense, and so the motion picture is not developed as an art form but as an eye teaser, a toy, a mechanism to puzzle, thrill and divert—but not to tell the truth, not to carry ideas as every art form that is real must carry ideas and so bring truth to the heart.

Of course, a few films are released, now and then, which allow the background to take its proper place as a medium of artistic effect. But they are so few that they stand out signally. I have before me a copy of the "Variety" which gives a Calendar of Current Releases. Out of a total of three hundred pictures released in the last four or five months about fifteen, or twenty at the utmost, could be recommended to the discriminating movie-goer. Possibly, the moron will walk out on those I recommend. He will wonder what they are all about, why something doesn't happen, and will say in the foyer of the theatre, "Well, what's the answer?" and walk away bewildered. But if pictures like "David Copperfield" and "Les Misérables" could come into the theatres where people might be regularly attracted and should continue attracted by the promise of pictures appealing as "David Copperfield" and "Les Misérables" appeal, to a reasonably high intelligence, the motion picture producer could annex an entirely new section of the population as patrons of the screen. But to produce, night after night, pictures of this high standard, the door keeper would have to bar the lowbrow.

Now, of course, in the ordinary motion-picture house a production of the best grade would not live long. But it is no sufficient answer to prove that an inferior movie lives longer than a good one and makes more money. It is not the contention of this thesis that the motion-picture producers do not know how to make more money out of the business than their critics would make following their own theories.

The contention of those who criticize the movie industry is that, in the managerial eagerness to make all the money possible all the time, the producers have degraded what might have been an art into something that is too often dull where it is not nasty, or, at best, a whirligig toy to dazzle idle minds.

The value of the discovery of the motion picture is cheapened by the kind of thing discovered. It offers a nervous relaxation for tired people. It is little better than chewing gum, in that. The whole vast movie industry, with its billions invested and with its hundreds of thousands employed, under the present status of production, distribution and exhibition, gives us little that is much better than a glittering toy for an imbecile giant.

CHAPTER II

THE MOTION PICTURE INDUSTRY

by

THE MOST REVEREND JOHN J. CANTWELL, D.D.

SOMETHING of the enormous popularity of the cinema may be gleaned from an examination of the attendance records of recent years. Previous to the advent of the present widespread industrial depression the figures for paid attendance at motion-picture theatres in the United States were in excess of 100 million a week. Even now, with more than nine million Americans said to be unemployed, with suffering and poverty and hunger widespread throughout the land, the attendance figures hover close to seventy million a week. It is estimated that world attendance upon American-made motion pictures at the present time is close to 250 million a week. The average price of admission throughout the world is about fourteen cents—the average price in the United States is about nineteen cents.

American producers of motion pictures produce each year more than eighty-four per cent of the world's product. The pictures made in the United States are generally accepted as the best from a technical, mechanical and dramatic standpoint, and thus it comes about that American-made pictures set the style in motion-picture production for all the world. Motion-picture producing companies everywhere seek to ape the Hollywood producers in the type and kind of screen fare offered for public approval.

Ninety per cent of all motion pictures made in the United States are made by eight producing companies, whose production headquarters are located in Hollywood. These eight companies, and a number of smaller units, are members of the "Hays Association," so-called—the Motion Picture Producers and Distributors of America, Inc., whose president is Will H. Hays, former Postmaster General of the United States, with offices in New York City and in Hollywood. A California corporation known as the Association of Motion Picture Producers, Inc., whose president is Louis B. Mayer (Vice-president of the Metro-Goldwyn-Mayer Corporation) is a subsidiary corporation of the Hays Association in New York. All the members of the Hollywood association are members of the association in New York. The Hollywood Association operates as a separate corporate entity but is dominated and controlled by the organization in New York.

About 480 feature-length talking motion pictures are made each year in the United States. Ninety-six per cent of these are made in Hollywood. In addition, the companies which are members of the Hays Association produce about 2,500 "shorts" each year—pictures of one or two reels made as entertainment pictures (not commercial or educational pictures) for exhibition in theatres.

In the production of these entertainment talking pictures about 100 million dollars is expended annually. Another 100 million dollars is spent each year in advertising these pictures, chiefly in the newspapers, and a third 100 million is spent in selling and distributing the pictures to the theatres. At the present time there are in the United States more than 16,000 motion picture theatres equipped for the projection of sound, or synchronized, motion pictures. Of this number more than 3,000 are closed at present, due to the widespread industrial depression.

Silent motion pictures for exhibition as entertainment in theatres are no longer being made. There is no market for these. When American-made talking pictures are sent abroad to countries where the common language is other than English, the pictures are shown either in versions into which the language of the country has been *dubbed* by a clever mechanical contrivance of synchronization, or the language coming from the screen is English with *printed dialogue* in the language of the country, superimposed upon the pictures. Thirty per cent of the gross revenue of all major producing companies in the United States comes from films sold and exhibited abroad.

There is much commercial rivalry throughout the world among producers of motion pictures. Until the advent of the talking picture the American product maintained almost a world monopoly. With the coming of sound, however, and the early difficulty caused by the language, producers in foreign countries (even in the British Empire) sought to build up their own production companies. In addition to the commercial advantages which it was hoped to secure by native production of pictures, a number of the foreign countries opposed the exhibition of American-made motion pictures on the ground that these were subversive of decency and public morality. In almost every country in the world a strict governmental censorship of motion pictures is maintained and many American pictures are rejected by these censors and not licensed for exhibition on the charge that these "are not suited for public exhibition."

In recent years—since 1929—the motion picture business in the United States, like most other industries which had been greatly developed during the period which followed the World War, has suffered considerable deflation.

The generally accepted explanation of this condition is: 1. the industrial depression which has affected seriously all industrial enterprise; 2. the wild scramble half a dozen years back on the part of all big companies to buy, or build, big motion-picture theatres in neighborhoods and in cities where there is no need for them. All the larger companies became seriously involved financially with these unnecessary and very costly theatres, built in an effort to stave off competition and to insure a market for the products of their studios. In the process of rehabilitation, now under way, or already completed, most of these unnecessary, or poorly situated theatres, either have been converted to other uses, or are standing idle. As a result of all this, millions upon millions of investors' dollars have been lost in the motion-picture industry.

Previous to the coming of the talking picture, the American-made motion pictures sinned chiefly because of its vulgarity. Occasionally, of course, a silent picture undertook to tell a story not suited for screen dramatization; frequently the old silent films offended by their suggestiveness. Some few were definitely vile. Against all such there began to grow half-a-dozen years back considerable public protest. This wave of condemnation had its inspiration chiefly from among organized groups of Protestant churchmen, and the Federal Council's of the Churches of Christ in America began actively to organize forces to oppose and drive out these wrong kinds of films. The Federal Council's work had hardly got under way in earnest when along came the talking motion picture. This, for a while, served as a great magnet for box-office attraction. The motion-picture producing companies, over night, reorganized their business and changed their films from silent to talking pictures, with tremendous profit to all concerned. The "talkies" were a novelty and theatre patrons in all parts of the world flocked by the millions to the movies.

With the coming of the talking picture has come greater and more far-reaching influence. The pictures now impress their patrons not only by sight but with animated sound as well. The talking picture broadened the field of the movies and opened up new channels of art and drama. Screen plays, lifted almost bodily from the fast-degenerating Broadway stage, were made into movies over night, with the result that the cinema has now become the instrument for the telling of tales the like of which was confined, a few years back, to the sophisticated stage or the barnyard.

The difficulties with the talking pictures as we now have them is that they have taken to preaching a philosophy of life which, in most instances, is definitely the wrong philosophy, sinister and insidious. The most competent authority in Hollywood to-day is responsible for the statement that many of the talking pictures made out there "teach the philosophy that marriage, the purity of women and the sanctity of the home are out-moded sentimentalities," unworthy of serious consideration at the hands of "intelligent" Americans.

The stories upon which most of the present-day movies are built concern themselves with a discussion of social problems. The movies now discuss morals, divorce, free love, race suicide, unborn children, sexual relationship outside marriage and "double standards," the relation of sex to religion, marriage and its effect "upon the freedom of women." These and a dozen other kindred subjects have been injected into the talking picture. There is no need to argue the effect of all this upon the public who witness them.

An examination of a number of the motion pictures recently released for public exhibition suggests that the entire motion-picture industry has set itself to the task of seeing which company can produce the most vicious films. In great numbers of these recently exhibited pictures there is a definite attempt to create audience sympathy for the violation of the moral law. The subject matter of most of these offensive films deals with sex relation of every conceivable kind. Sin is condoned, false moral values are instilled in young and critical minds and thus are lowered both the public and the private standards of conduct of all who see them. When the pictures are not vile *in toto*—the subject matter, presentation, photography, dialogue, action—the films are crowded with salacious details, smutty talk, obscene wit, offensive situ-

ations. If one were to glean one's knowledge of family
life in America from the American screen presentation,
one would, unerringly, come to believe that adultery is
but a slight adventure in romance that any understanding
wife should easily forgive. It goes without saying that
a number of the films attempt to justify adultery, while
sexual irregularities are played up with enthusiasm and
made to appear as acceptable and defensible. A number
of pictures selected at random from recent releases measure up something like this: *one* is based upon seduction,
rape and prostitution; *two* had a foreign—South Sea
Isle—locale and offended by a plot embracing aphro-
disiac drugs, rape and revenge; the *third,* also a picture
with foreign locale, was based upon a romance of native
toxicology and nudity; a *fourth* is the story of a nudist
colony which, so far, a number of the political censor
boards have refused to license for public exhibition; a
fifth was a violently revolting story of a mother who became a prostitute in order to provide luxury and education for her son; a *sixth* deals with an alleged cultured
social worker who makes it a practice to bear children
to men she never sees afterward, the while the "cultured"
lady attains great distinction in the field of social welfare
and betterment; the *seventh* contributed a new study to
the unhappy small-town girl made happy by the gay ad-
venturer from the city—she giving him her body "on
call"; the *eighth* was concerned with the lechery of a
fanatic monk and his two attempts at rape; the *ninth*
was a rowdy farce with Boccacian dialogue; in the *tenth,*
adultery was justified, or at least conveniently forgotten
in discussion which sought to show that a man's mistress

can be his wife more truly "in the sight of God" than the
woman he married.

One of the recently released films provides a combina-
tion of horror and sex which is startling and nauseating;
another, based upon the early days of Christianity, featured an erotic dance that gave great offence to patrons in
all parts of the world; still another was the familiar
"kept-woman" drama in which the heroine justified her
actions to her mother with the simple explanation "I
love him." This same moral principle that deep human
affection is an adequate excuse for incontinence, was also
preached to the youth of the land by another outstanding
"hit" of the current season.

Not all talking motion pictures made in the United
States are based upon gross sexual irregularities. Probably
one-fourth of them is entitled to be so classified. Many of
the pictures are based upon details which may well incite
to crime. Some of them make a point of glorifying not
only the harlot but her gangster "boy-friend" as well.
But, for all practical purposes, it may be well sustained
that *twenty-five per cent of all pictures made in Hollywood in the course of a year are definitely bad and offensive.*

Now, it may be asked, who is responsible for all this
vileness and worse, that is being made to serve as the instrument of debauchery of the youth of the land?

The actors, as such, have little influence on the character
of the stories that are placed upon the screen. Players
are not usually consulted regarding the moral values, or
lack of them, that a type or character which they may be
called upon to play, suggests. Along with the director

of the picture, the writer is the person who creates all the filth of the pictures and it is the writer who is most responsible, next to the managing executives of the studios. With the coming of the talkies there went to Hollywood hundreds of playwrights from the Broadway stage, authors of vaudeville skits and acts and playlets. Along with these went the authors of current "literary" successes, the writers of the pornographic school whose books have had a great sale in recent years. It is from these men and women that the stories now current on the screen are selected. *Seventy-five per cent of these authors are pagans.* They are men and women who care nothing for decency, good taste or refinement. Most of them are living lives of infidelity and worse, wherein there is to be found not a suggestion of respect for religion or for spiritual values.

Someone has taken occasion to say recently that "all the worthwhile literary talent in the world" hovers near to Hollywood. In large measure this is true, if by literary talent you mean those men and women whose works appear to have a popular appeal. And if this be true, then one cannot help but observe that the world of literature to-day is in a bad way. If this be literature, then write it down that we are in the midst of an almost universal era of cynicism, obscenity and destructive criticism. Our writers for the screen spend much of their talents glorifying the female libertine and the public prostitute. As panderers of this sort, our motion-picture producers have welcomed them and shifted the blame to the public, with the excuse that the public wants that sort of story and will have no other.

It is true in a measure that this sort of stuff seems to be the stuff that American audiences want. What a sad commentary all this is on our literary achievements! After a hundred and fifty years of our boasted education, free and untrammeled, our people care for nothing higher than the vapers of the pig-sty!

Dr. Hamlin Garland in a recently-published book of reminiscences, speaking of the present condition of our literary school, must have had our motion-picture writers in mind when he wrote:

> Another and still more disturbing change is in process. New York is becoming each year more European, more antagonistic to what certain of its writers call New England Puritanism. Month by month these people, contemptuous of "the American tradition," join in celebrating the novelists and dramatists who sound the sexual note most insistently. A claque for the pornographic has developed. It is becoming fashionable to sneer at marriage, chastity, home life, the church, and to bring into the dining-room the jokes and "wise-cracks" of the roadhouse. Certain so-called philosophers openly advocate the morals of the barnyard, in their essays on "freedom" and their attacks on "the Puritanical ideal." Others have achieved a success by the cheap and easy device of building stories of the saloon and the brothel. . . . This is the most disturbing phase of the whole situation. Young writers, perceiving that the pornographic experts are the highest-paid men and women in the field of authorship, are led to write their confessions and voice their "defiances."

In any discussion having to do with moral values in motion-picture entertainment it is the practice with many of the producing people in Hollywood to point to the box-office success of pictures which, to many patrons, are definitely offensive. As a matter of fact, the records indicate that few pictures that are vile, suggestive or unclean attain to any outstanding success. True, a great number of indecent pictures have some fair measure of success, just as certain popular novels of the present day seem to attain to some success if they are what Bill Nye used to designate as "spicy." But as with novels, so with the screen plays: the great outstanding successes are as clean as a hound's tooth. The most popular screen players to-day are identified with clean, wholesome entertainment.

The most outstandingly successful screen offering of the current season is a cartoon comedy in color entitled "Three Little Pigs," with not a shadow of suggestiveness about it. The most successful musical screen play is a foreign picture entitled "Be Mine To-night." "Cavalcade," the stirring screen play produced by the Fox Company almost a year ago, at a cost in excess of one million dollars, continues, in all parts of the world, to sweep everything before it. At the present time there are several fine, clean pictures current in the theatres and they are doing an exceptionally good business.

On the other hand, from an authoritative source comes the information that of a group of "26 over-sexed pictures made this year, only two have been 'outstanding official successes.' One is rated as 'good'; another as 'not so good.' Nine were only fair box-office successes." This, it is suggested, gives no substance to the contention that "dirt" on the screen is profitable.

The chief difficulty with the production end of the motion-picture industry is that there are too many of the wrong kind of people engaged in it. The production of motion pictures, after all, is a definite form of art, and the films reflect unerringly the moral character of those who create the pictures. One cannot expect a man who has no appreciation of decency or cleanliness, himself, to be very much concerned with the importance of making his picture clean and decent and wholesome. One whose normal antennae are attuned to the mouthings of the gutter, is not likely to react favorably to the wholesome atmosphere of the higher strata. And just so long as those wrong kinds of people are in a position to control the moral content of the motion picture, just so long will the filth of the screen continue.

It is important to note again that not all motion pictures are bad. Many of them are; a substantial portion of them is not. In an effort to stamp out the wrong kind of pictures, the members of the Motion Picture Producers and Distributors of America in 1931 adopted and formally signed a document that has come to be known as the "Hays Moral Code." This document was written by a Catholic priest, the Rev. Daniel A. Lord, S.J., of St. Louis, Mo. All the larger producers of talking motion pictures in the United States are signatories to this Code, as are many of the smaller producers. Under Hays' jurisdiction, a bureau was set up in the Hollywood offices of the Association of Motion Picture Producers, Inc., to see to the task of applying the very excellent principles of the "Hays Moral Code" to the production of pictures. Colonel Jason S. Joy was placed in charge of this work and for a while a successful effort was made to conform the pictures to the Code. Unfortunately, however, this good work did not last long. Steadily, during the past two or three years the regulations of the Code have been "honored more in the breach than in the observance," with the result that a new and complete overhauling is now imperative if the motion-picture industry is to survive unhampered by additional State censorship bodies or a Federal censorship law. As this is written, there is no knowledge of what the National Government, by way of the N.R.A., may do regarding the moral values of screen entertainment, though it is reasonable to expect that the Federal Government will not shut its eyes completely to this most important phase of the industry's problems. Certain it is that some action of heroic proportions must be taken if we are to save the youth of America from a pollution and debauchery the like of which America has never known heretofore. In vain do we struggle to rear great educational institutions, if the invidious character of the cinema is permitted to prostitute the character of our adolescent youth. So great is the power of the motion picture to impress the youth of the land that one hour spent in the darkness of a cinema palace, intent on the unfolding of a wrong kind of story, can and frequently does nullify years of careful training on the part of the Church, the school, the home. So great is the problem suggested by the wrong kind of talking picture that drastic efforts must be launched at once if we are to stave off national disaster.

CHAPTER III

THE MOVIES, THE ACTOR, AND PUBLIC MORALS

by

EDWARD G. ROBINSON

THE actor who takes himself and his work seriously is not concerned with morals. In view of the fact that morality is usually applied to "the conduct of other people," it already has more watch dogs than necessary for its preservation. It is the exclusive business of reformers, preachers, grammarians and legislators. And therein, perhaps, lies the root of all evil. The cry for cleaner pictures, for cleaner stage, art and literature, has been made a business of. The actor, not unlike all true artists, is primarily interested in rendering a faithful portrayal of the part he undertakes. If he is called upon to interpret the role of a villain, he must not shrink from accentuating the propensities or idiosyncracies of that particular character no matter how hideous or despicable. To impersonate an underworld character requires as much histrionic ability as to enact the part of saint or nobleman. Most important is to render the character lifelike and human, and if necessary, repulsive and grotesque.

Good and evil, vice and virtue, saint and sinner, have no place in the lexicon of the artist. They are purely the concepts of moralists. "Art," says Romain Rolland, "is a comet sweeping through the infinite. It may be that its force is useful; it may be that it is apparently useless and dangerous in the existing order of the work-a-day world, but it is a force—it is movement and force, it is the lightning from heaven and for that very reason it is beneficent—it is like the sun from whence it has sprung. The sun is neither moral nor immoral. It is that which is; it lights the darkness of space. *And so does art."*

I realize that I lay myself open to severe criticism, and, possibly, even to ridicule and scorn by my daring presumption that the movies, or any phase of activity connected with them, have any kinship to art. The movies have been rocked in a cradle of sordid commercialism and have been dubbed an "industry." The vast majority of people attending them fails to appreciate the various branches of art that enter into the making of a simple, single reel. I shall discuss the "commercial" and "industrial" aspects of the cinema later. But whatever negative influence those aspects may have, I can still say without fear of contradiction that the movies have surrounded themselves with the most gifted of artists. There is no locality in the world that can boast of a finer aggregate of talent than Hollywood—not even barring Vienna. Every European country has its art ambassadors in Hollywood, representing every form of art—acting, directing, writing, painting. Romain Rolland's definition of art and the inference I have drawn from it, are, therefore, not so far fetched.

I do not wish to appear academic and indulge in hair splitting polemics, but even an actor must be logical when he lays aside his makeup and undertakes to wield the pen.

If, then, we define art as a force "that lights the darkness of space," a force that may be either "useful" or "useless," "beneficent" or injurious, constructive or destructive, moral or immoral, none but one who has an ax to grind would protest against the portrayal of underworld characters on the screen. Human beings, with few exceptions, are no paragons of virtue. There is something detestable in the best of us and something admirable in the worst of us. And if "Little Caesars" exist in life why not depict them on the screen or stage?

The moralist's objection to "Little Caesar," and to pictures of a similar *genre,* was that a hero has been made out of a rapscallion, that an enemy of society has been endowed with certain redeeming features, with certain laudatory traits, and that when he met the doom he so justly deserved, he evoked a sympathetic response from the human breast. That may be true. But there is no gainsaying that "Little Caesar," and many of his phototypes in the underworld, have a code of morals of their own. They evince a loyalty among themselves seldom encountered among men in our so-called upper strata of society. A dangerous assertion for a respectable citizen to make, no doubt; but to state a fact does not necessarily mean its endorsement. It is a well known fact that Arnold Rothstein and "Legs" Diamond and many other notorious criminals had met death at the hands of their own henchmen; and yet, when questioned by the police before they died, these victims had steadfastly refused to divulge the names of their assailants, though they knew the hand that had pulled the trigger.

"Little Caesar" was, in the parlance of gangdom "a

square shooter." His ambition was to become czar of his immediate underworld. In the light of the milieu to which he belonged and, perhaps, even in our own light, he was kind, generous, and on the level,—a real pal to his faithful hangers on. But woe to him who double crossed him. Born and bred in a different environment, he probably would have turned out to be a useful member of society. However, be that as it may. It is unreasonable to assume that the character of "Little Caesar" was glorified in any form, shape or manner. His miserable end precluded any such conclusion. He died like a rat. The picture pointed to a definite moral: He who lives by the sword shall die by it, or, the wages of sin is death.

In my opinion, the success of "Little Caesar" was due to the fact that the character was truly conceived and drawn by the author. If he were not human and lifelike he would have not appealed to the multitudes. The vogue of any novel, play or movie, depends entirely upon the human elements with which the protagonist has been invested. Life is, for the most part, drab and monotonous. People read books and go to the theatre to temporarily forget their immediate surroundings—house, duties, children, husbands, wives, responsibilities. By following the exploits of the hero or heroine of a good story we experience a vicarious thrill. If the characters are faithfully drawn we often change places with them. How many of us wanted but lacked the courage to emulate the pleasant wickedness of the characters flashed before us on the screen? We are fed up with being constantly good. Virtue may have its reward in heaven, but why wait so long if vice has its own charms and pays dividends here and now?

If we do not follow the paths of "Little Caesar," it is not because we are virtuous but because we are intelligent, or, maybe, because we fear the policeman, or St. Peter, or our own conscience. Secretly most of us applaud those who dare and do. To illustrate this unconsciously hidden admiration each and every one has for the delinquents of society, I can do no better than to relate the following story:

One day, as I walked out of a picture house (yes, I go to the movies quite often, and not always to see the pictures in which I appear), I was confronted by an elderly woman who was leading a seven or eight year old boy by the hand. She asked me if I was Edward G. Robinson. I admitted my identity.

"So it's you who played 'Little Caesar' and so many other bad men?" She said more in the form of reproof than seeking information.

I pleaded guilty to the accusation.

"Well, I'm glad I have this opportunity of telling you to your face what a bad influence your pictures have had on our young people."

"What makes you think so?" I asked her.

"I ought to know," she replied quite sure of her ground, "I've taken my grandchild to see 'Little Caesar' eight times."

I sincerely hope that all the sins committed by the "bad men" I have played will not be chalked up against me. Nor do I want it understood that I am particularly fond of, or hold a brief for, gangsters, killers and the vanishing bootlegger. My neighbors will vouch that I am a peaceful citizen and an honest taxpayer. I even observe all traffic regulations. Nevertheless, I would like to know and understand the psychology of the criminals that fill our prisons. I would like to probe the mainsprings of the human soul that make one a saint and another a sinner. Freud blames our anti-social vagaries on the "infantile" and "primitive" instincts forever lurking in the "subconscious," and waiting for the opportunity to overpower us. We never can tell when these monsters might break loose and turn us into criminals.

It is all too engrossing a subject, criminology is. And my interest in it is purely professional. I believe that it is impossible for any actor to render a true portrayal of character unless he can fathom the psychology that prompts a man to do the stupidest things.

I have often wondered why it is that our moral preachers, forever trying to reform this sinful world of ours, have never turned their broadside against the press. The fables presented on the screen are Sunday School sermons compared to some of the stories featured in our dailies. As an example, let us glance at the records dealing with the shooting of John Dillinger.

That that event was an important news item is undeniable; and no one can take exception to the detailed description of the various incidents leading to the apprehension and killing of Public Enemy Number I featured in the newspapers. It was a fine piece of detective work—intelligent, daring, well-planned and well-executed. But was it necessary to go into detail about Dillinger's life, his habits, his criminal exploits, his love affairs and his burial? Column after column was devoted to the gunman even for days after the shooting. If a movie were made of the actual newspaper records, our moralists would have denounced it as indecent, tending to corrupt the morals of the young. But an even more egregious breach of good taste committed by the press and condoned by the champions of public morals is still fresh in our memory.

No event in the annals of recent history has been more publicized than the Hauptmann case. No details of the court proceedings, fit or unfit for public consumption, were omitted. Every bit of testimony was faithfully recorded. Full page photographs of all the *dramatis personæ* connected with the trial were displayed. Every prominent newspaper featured special articles by specially assigned correspondents. The world's literati were gathered in the courtroom at Flemington, N. J. Every move and gesture of the defendant were dwelt upon. How and what he ate, how he slept, and the mood he was in at the various stages of the trial. In addition to all these minutae covered by the press, every radio station had special commentators analyzing and dissecting the evidence. Motion pictures, showing the defendant on the witness stand, were surreptitiously taken and shown on the screen twenty-four hours later. If ever an arch criminal was lionized it was Hauptmann.

Turn to the pages of the tabloids, the circulation of which, in round numbers, rivals the movie-going public. How much space do they devote to politics, to international affairs, to scientific discoveries, to civic and cultural progress? Hardly any. But a mere rumor that

a Hollywood star is about to be divorced will be featured
in type a foot high.

The tendency of the press to stress the sensational may
be multiplied *ad infinitum.* Gruesome stories of murder,
arson and rape, salacious accounts of divorce cases and
breach of promise suits, so boldly related as to leave
nothing to the imagination, have always been featured by
the newspapers. Let us turn to the newspaper files of
bygone years and note the news items that were given
prominence: The homicide trials of Harry Thaw, Nan
Patterson, Rolland Molyneux, the Becker case, Ruth
Snyder. City editors know their business. They know the
importance of news value. They know that their readers
love melodrama. And what is more melodramatic than
a man or woman being tried for murder?

The advocates of movie censorship maintain that the
general, present day disregard for law and order has been
enhanced by the screen's exploitation of scandalous and
unsavory topics. Are we then to assume that the sordid
stories flashed on the front pages of our dailies exert a
more benign influence than the fictitious and highly
romantic tales flashed on the screen? That is hardly conceivable.

Apparently, the attitude of our moralists towards the
press, on the one hand, and the movies, on the other, is
somewhat paradoxical. And there is only one plausible
explanation for this paradox. The Fourth Estate is too
dangerous, and a much too powerful an organization to
attack. The movies provide a less dangerous target. And
besides, even reformers crave publicity. It would not do
to war against the press.

In my opinion, neither the movies nor the press can be held reprehensible for the widespread of lawlessness and the laxity of morals. If our would be censors were better sociologists, and more concerned with truth than with morals, they would experience no difficulty in giving us a correct diagnosis of the symptoms.

Every literature and every art reflects its own age. Underlying Aeschylus, Sophocles and Euripides appears the fatalism of the ancient Greek religion. Underlying Michael Angelo, Leonardo da Vinci and Boticelli appears the pagan ideal of the strong and happy man of the Renaissance bent upon the pursuit of his desires. Underlying the poetry and drama of the Elizabethan age appears the ideal so immortally invested in the words of the Bard of Avon:

> ". . . To thine own self be true,
> And it must follow, as the night the day,
> Thou canst not be false to any man."

Similarly, underlying the art and literature of our own day appears a philosophy cynical and destructive, a philosophy stripped of all the ideals man has cherished since the dawn of the Christian era, a philosophy that was negated by the perpetration of every conceivable, human indecency during the world war, and the supposedly Garden of Eden that man has for centuries tried to cultivate suddenly assumed the aspect of an African jungle, only infinitely more ruthless. Man forgot the very existence of the Ten Commandments.

Between 1914 and 1918 millions of the flower of the

world's youth were sacrificed to Moloch. Men were taught to shoot, and were honored, decorated and glorified for killing their fellow men. Women were shamed and outraged, babies starved and mutilated. In face of such horrors honor and virtue became meaningless. If murder *en masse* is sanctioned by political, religious and civic leaders in time of war, why is it criminal to shoot down a couple of individuals in time of peace? Little wonder that many of our boys turned into desperados, and many of our girls dispensed with the virtue their mothers had known. Life has become spectacular and melodramatic, and truth has actually become stranger than fiction. In recent years the columns of our dailies have been more exciting than the most thrilling detective stories. Not long ago a New York newspaper featured a story of a holdup that took place in an office directly above a motion picture theatre where a capacity audience followed intently the flickering shadows on the screen—"unaware," commented the reporter, "that something more thrilling than what they were seeing at the moment was taking place overhead." Indeed, reality transcends imagination.

Prohibition, too, has put a crimp into our social order. The Eighteenth Amendment was the greatest villain of modern times. It was the instigator of corruption, intemperance, malfeasance, gunplay and terrorism. The bootlegger was the progenitor of the gangster, and both the immediate progeny of the enactment of an unnatural law. The bootlegger and the gangster fortuitously, and ironically enough, became the champions of liberty, a sort of knight errants clothed in sham glamour and romanticism.

No, neither the press nor the movies can be held reprehensible for the bold defiance of our laws—state, federal
and church. It is our social and economic upheaval that
has robbed man of his illusions and made him revert to
the "infantile" and "primitive." The movies of the last
few years have only mirrored the disintegration of civilization; they have not initiated it.

My personal aversion to censorship and my dislike for
its sponsors must not, however, be misinterpreted as an
unqualified endorsement of all screen entertainment. I
take exception to many of the things producers will do in
the hope of turning out a successful picture. But my
reservations are based on the artistic rather than the moral
side of the question.

Despite the fact that the actor and the producer have a
common objective, that is, to interest and amuse the
public, they not infrequently clash about the methods
employed in obtaining that objective. The actor's
primary concern is to render an honest and sincere
portrayal of the part entrusted to him. He will intuitively
recoil from the inconsistencies of character extemporized
by the haphazard events of a story that has no verisimili-
tude to life. Unfortunately, too many such stories find
their way to the screen, and the actors appearing in them
are not at all happy. To be sure, those who have
clambered to the highest rung of the professional ladder
are allowed more or less leeway in the choosing of
their own screen material. But that does not obviate the
difficulties confronting the movie industry as a whole in
the selection of its screen material.

The actor, too, apart from his own artistic integrity, must keep faith with his public. The public is quick to sense an insincere and makeshift characterization, and will not hesitate to repudiate the actor that undertakes it, even though he be their favorite. What P. T. Barnum said about fooling the people still holds good, and not a few actors have lost out with the public just for that reason. The psychology governing audiences in the theatre is peculiar. Individually their opinions may or may not be correct. But collectively their judgment is infallible. It is for this very reason that I feel that the public is capable of choosing its own screen entertainment without the guidance of self appointed moralists. An audience is intuitively repelled by a play, movie or novel that is suggestive and prurient without rhyme or reason. Both theatrical and motion picture producers have learned this lesson to the detriment of their pocket books.

But I have somewhat digressed. I was going to discuss the problems of the motion picture producer.

Compared to the producer's task the actor's is simple indeed. The so-called screen star is called upon to make three or at most four pictures a year. But when we stop to consider that each major studio in Hollywood turns out between forty-eight and sixty features annually, a combined output of about four hundred, exclusive of the three score or more filmed by the independent companies, we can readily appreciate the magnitude of the producer's job in the selection and choice of screen material to cover his production schedule. The demand for good original stories is greater than the supply. This is evidenced by the fabulous sums paid by studios for successful plays and novels. To meet the shortage of desirable screen fare studios must rely upon their own staff of writers. And although there is no dearth of talent among them, the synthetic or made to order fables usually lack spontaneity, and not infrequently are dull and stupid.

The reason for the difference of opinion arising between actor and producer is now obvious. The producer works according to schedule. He must turn out so many pictures a year. He cannot pay attention to the complaints of the actor who is solely concerned with his own part. If he had the time he probably would, but his main interest is centered on providing an evenly diverting screen entertainment, and he must subordinate the wishes of the individual actor to what he believes to be the good of the picture as a whole.

A remedy for this malady is easy to prescribe, but somewhat difficult to shove it down the patient's throat. Studios should operate on a smaller production schedule. Instead of sixty pictures annually no studio should undertake an output of more than twenty.

Unfortunately, the business of making films, which is really a great art, has been reduced to the level of an "industry." Studios must be run on the profit and loss system. Hundreds of millions of dollars are invested in "lots," sound stages, equipment, and what not. Stockholders demand dividends. The machinery must be kept in motion day and night. There is no let up. Actors, directors, cameramen, technicians, have been known to work fifteen and sixteen hours a day for a number of consecutive days when a picture in the making was behind schedule.

Haste is not conducive to art. Art and commercialism are deadly enemies, always were and always will be. And yet, despite this incompatibility, Hollywood has managed to provide screen entertainment that compares most favorably to the best produced in European countries.

There is, however, one phase of commercialism that might be easily dispensed with without much loss to the studios or their stars. I mean the exploitation of the private lives of screen personalities—though a gradual diminution of this practice has of late become noticeable.

The practice of bringing to the fore and stressing the intimate lives of screen stars has been more or less responsible for the opprobrium heaped upon the movies. If one were to judge Hollywood by the fan magazines, and no doubt millions of people do or did, one would imagine that screen stars are always lounging around in costly negligees or pajamas, attending parties and getting drunk nightly, and constantly changing husbands and wives. Having a one track mind, moralists will confound the scandal they read about a particular screen personality with the character that that particular individual happens to portray. If, for example, Virginia Quelquesfois has been twice married and divorced, that is legally speaking, how can she possibly play the part of a virtuous woman, and how can the picture in which she appears be possibly "clean?" And the reverse is, of course, also true. How can Miss Quelquesfois possibly be virtuous if she plays the part of an immoral woman in an immoral movie? All of which is the result of misdirected publicity, of exploiting the feminine angle instead of the actress and artist.

This exploitation of the person rather than the profession, of individual traits and habits rather than talent, of charm rather than ability, applies particularly to the female contingent of the screen. And I know that this sort of ballyhoo is personally distasteful to them. And it is not at all necessary.

What, for instance, does the theatre going public of New York, Chicago and Boston know about the private lives of Katherine Cornell, Eva Le Galliene or Lynn Fontaine? I doubt if it is aware that Miss Cornell is wed to Guthrie McClintic, or that Miss Galliene has never been married, or that Miss Fontaine sleeps in a nightgown or pajamas. The public only knows that they are great artists, and it is mostly interested in their professional careers. The public will long remember Miss Cornell's impersonation of Elizabeth Browning in "The Barretts of Wimpole Street," nor will it ever forget Miss Le Galliene's work at the Civic Repertory Theatre, nor Miss Fontaine's long and brilliant association with the Theatre Guild.

And that is all the theatre going public should know about any actress or actor—their professional careers. And that is all I would like the movie going public to know about our Hollywood stars—to know them and judge them by their work on the screen, by their portrayal of difficult roles; in brief, by the triumphs they have achieved as artists.

Yes, I am afraid Hollywood has done many things in poor taste. Withal, it is just as "clean" as Seventh Avenue, or Tudor City, or as any other cross section of our American Metropolis taken at random.

It has been generally assumed that the present tendency of the movies towards the classics and history has been prompted by the drive for cleaner screen diversion. Nothing is so wide off the mark. The studios, I believe, have no apologies to make for their past performances. Their objective always was, and will no doubt remain, to provide entertainment for those who seek it. And in this respect they have not failed the public. But the present trend towards the classics and history came about quite accidentally.

A little over a year ago a major studio filmed a classical novel. Audiences everywhere responded to it. And inasmuch as producers usually endeavor to give the public what it wants, they turned to other classical novels. So far so good. Tomorrow this trend may change. But tomorrow will take care of itself. And so will the public, without the aid of professional reformers to tell it what it should reject or accept.

CHAPTER IV

THE EDUCATIONAL SIGNIFICANCE OF THE MOVIES

by

RAYMOND J. CANNON

A COLLEGE professor, whose name I do not recall, defined education as the process of drawing out one's potentialities so as to live in harmony with one's environment. I like this definition very much. It does not limit education to school curriculums and book knowledge. It embraces all human experience.

In the light of this definition, the educative force of the movies cannot be overestimated. The movies are ubiquitous. The world is their classroom, and every man, woman and child, their pupils. It is unfortunate that they have not utilized their opportunities to better advantage. What a sorry and sordid jumble so many pictures of late have turned out to be! With the whole field of literature at its disposal, the motion-picture industry has degenerated into the mere demoralizing depicturization of debased events.

We may be somewhat tardy in taking up the subject of "clean" movies. On the other hand, it is never too late to improve. It is high time that a nation, yes, a world wide interest, should be shown in the selection and exhibition of pictures that we and our families are likely to see.

Much has been said about the influence which the movies have had upon the private lives of the people of this country. And yet it is obvious that not enough has been said or can be said until sufficient sentiment has been aroused in the minds of the majority of the people of this and every other nation to instill into the motion-picture world the idea of the necessity of "decent" pictures, or no box office receipts.

We, as an enlightened people, have been extremely lax upon this subject. We have permitted our children to see anything and everything which the movie world produced. How can we too strongly condemn the censorship boards when we, ourselves, have been so careless? Nevertheless, there is much to be said upon this subject. It is the duty of the censorship boards to pass upon the kind of pictures that are fit for our people, old and young, to see. There is no doubt that they have been grossly negligent in this respect. We should have been able to rely on their judgment, but that judgment has been faulty to the extreme.

The educational value of the movies has, to a great extent, been relegated to the scrap heap. If we were to accept the life and environment of the characters shown on the screen, in the last few years, as a guide, organized society and civilization would be bankrupt, and anarchy and chaos would prevail. The movies have seemed to delight in depicting some uncouth situation and playing it up in great style. This, in many instances, has been the worst kind of an education our children could get. The glorified gangster, the woman of no virtue, the hideously deformed body and brain—such was the stuff with which the movies regaled our eyes and ears. The best that can be said of the movies of recent years, with respect to education, is, that the physical background and color, of some of the period pictures, have given us an idea of how certain generations lived.

I have a very clear recollection of the advertising that was given a certain picture which John Dillinger was said to have seen just prior to his being killed by our Federal agents. In the city where I reside one theatre promptly secured the picture for a showing, and advertised it greatly in connection with the Dillinger case. It was referred to as the "gangster picture Dillinger saw just before he was shot." I was amazed at the crowds that were morbidly gazing at the display advertising outdoors while they were waiting to get into the picture house— crowds not only of adults, but of boys and girls in their teens. The only excuse for a gangster picture is, not to show what a wonderfully fascinating life the members of the underworld lead, or what excitement they have, or what wealth they surreptitiously acquire, but to show that crime does not pay.

Why should we show our children the ways of gangland? Of what educational value are such movies? Why incite our youth with the glamour of luxury attained by unlawful means? Crime is sufficiently rampant without making it an attractive game. To fill the heads of our youngsters with the thought that a life of wealth and ease may be secured so easily is positively dangerous. Far better would it be to encourage the thought that an honest livelihood outranks the comforts secured by dishonest means. Far be it from me to suggest a "Pollyanna" sort of movie. I do not advocate that our children should be wrapped in celophane. By all means let them be schooled in the arena of life, train them to differentiate between wrong and right, but let us not give them a wrong impression of values.

We must admit that the press has done much to suggest the glory of motion picture stars. It has almost come to the point where anything a "star" does is all right. "The king can do no wrong." A slight glimpse into the private lives of many of the so-called "stars" would soon convince one that if they had been living in any respectable, middle-class community outside of Hollywood, they would be outside the pale of "decent" society. This idea of idealizing and idolizing a certain individual for the simple reason that he or she gave a good characterization of some moron in a picture that had great box-office success, lends to our young people the thought that the private lives of our "stars" are above reproach, no matter what degree of moral laxity they subscribe to.

How frequently do we hear of the marriage of an actor or an actress, and how long does it last? A few months, a few years at most, and then, divorce. Rapidly, a new marriage, a new divorce—time and again. Legalized vice, that is all it is. "Till death do us part," should have some meaning. And outside of Hollywood, it still has, I am happy to say. The idea of changing partners constantly may be appropriate at a dance, but it is not quite so dignified in married life. The stability of the home and the family should be emphasized, even among "stars."

Home and family are the bulwarks of civilization. Even Communistic Russia has come to this realization, though, at first, it tried to disintegrate the institution of marriage. If we are to respect the movies we must respect the people who make them, and if we are to respect the people who make them we must respect the movies. Judging by past records, we can, unfortunately, respect neither.

To curb the salacious movies and to rid the profession of questionable actors, I introduced a Bill into Congress. It prohibits the transporting, interstate or international, of any moving picture in which "any of the persons taking part in the film have ever been arrested or convicted of any offense involving moral turpitude; or the actions of the persons taking part in the film are suggestive, unwholesome, and morally objectionable," and provides a fine or imprisonment as punishment for a transgression against the same. I firmly believe that such a Bill enacted into law will minimize the number of objectionable pictures produced, and that it will practically prevent their widespread distribution. It will also consummate the real ability of the true artist. This Bill enacted into law will segregate the mediocre from the great or near great. It will enable actors and actresses, who have genuine ability, to become affiliated with, and spend their talents on, an industry that will transfer to the screen characters and scenes that will hold the interest of, and be of considerable educational value to, both adults and children.

The improvement in the subject matter used for the screen would be notable. It is greatly desired that some such action should be taken. The low standard of pictures of late years has been a disgrace. The world's literature

affords the producers a wide field from which to choose
their material, and there is no reason why a suitable
variety of pictures should not be made. The trend, as
already indicated by the last few offerings, will undoubtedly be towards pictures based upon historical
events, or the classics, or other notable modern con-
tributions of letters.

There are numerous men and women in the movie industry at present who would in no way be affected by the
Bill I have proposed in Congress. Their performances
have always been of a high standard. They insist that
any picture in which they appear be truly "decent."
Perhaps the most widely known and loved actor in this
connection is the great GEORGE ARLISS. An Arliss
picture can be seen and enjoyed at any time by any one,
young or old. His pictures have a spirit of wholesome-
ness which is never lost. His characterizations are in-
imitable. Although an English gentleman and artist, we
more than welcome him to the American motion-picture
industry, and trust that he may remain here.

The Barrymores, Ethel, Lionel and John, are other
artists who can always be enjoyed. The characterizations
of Lionel Barrymore are superb. His younger brother
falls not far behind that high standard. The great Ethel
is incomparable. Too bad we do not see her more often
on the screen. But it is noteworthy that Arliss and the
Barrymores are products of the stage. So was the illustri-
ous late Marie Dressler. I am afraid it will be long before
some one will be found to step into the shoes of this
superb commedienne.

Leslie Howard is another screen actor recruited from

the stage. His work with Norma Shearer in "Smilin' Through" will linger long in one's memory. It is regrettable that Miss Shearer is not cast always in such charming pictures.

The movies made by Charles Chaplin have both interest, pathos and comedy. The world at large awaits his pictures impatiently. There are other pictures, few and far between, to be sure, to which the producers may point with pride. "Treasure Island" with Jackie Cooper, is one. And there was Cecil de Mille's "King of Kings." Did any picture surpass this in gate receipts? Why cannot we have more of the same kind?

The value of such movies is unquestioned. Their splendid educational value is undoubted. We await with interest the screen version of "David Copperfield." It should be a notable production, and we predict a record breaking run for it.

Viewing the situation from all angles, there seems to be no good reason why the motion picture industry, with all the money and facilities at its command, cannot be called upon to produce a generally higher level of pictures and held to strict responsibility if it falls below that level. This, however, in my estimation, will not be needed. The agitation has made the producers realize that the public cannot be trifled with. And the new output of pictures from Hollywood gives us every indication that we may hope and expect to see on the screen, day after day, movies that will be amusing, instructive and inspiring. There is no limit to the heights to which the industry may climb. Movies in the past have always been money makers. If crowds filled the theatres when cheap and tawdry movies were exhibited, there is every reason to believe that when the outstanding productions will appear the sign S.R.O. will be displayed in front of every motion-picture house.

By all means, let us not falter by the wayside. On the contrary, let us continue to fight for improvements in the movies which are offered for our diversion. If we persist, we will win. Better pictures—not sometimes, but always.

CHAPTER V

THE MOVIES AND JUVENILE DELINQUENCY

by

BEN B. LINDSEY

It is very difficult to enter into a frank discussion of the influence of moving pictures upon modern youth without being misunderstood. But after more than a quarter of a century as a judge of a Juvenile Court, and taking part in the promotion and establishment of such courts in practically every state in the Union, I cannot agree with what seems to me to be the extravagant claims of some of the critics of the movies. I refer to some of those who seem actually to insist that most crime among modern youth is due to what is shown in motion pictures.

While, of course, some young people have doubtless been encouraged in delinquencies by what they have seen in the movies, the same thing might be said of what they have read in the newspapers, magazines or books.

A very good argument could be made against the use of automobiles, because there isn't any doubt in my mind that the freedom they have brought to modern youth in bringing them together under conditions that—without chaperonage—in past generations would have been considered shocking, has contributed probably more to sex delinquency among youth than most any other cause. When we add the frightful toll of the dead and wounded thousands of youth from the reckless use or misuse of this useful contribution that the machine age has given to civilization, we might, in the interest of morality, find as much cause for boycotting automobiles as we would find for boycotting movies. And I am not saying that the boycotting of certain types of moving pictures would not be a very good thing; for I have given generous credit to the good influence of religious and ethical organizations who have in many cases justly opposed the evil influences of some motion pictures by resort to just such a remedy.

Good and evil is a matter of relativity. It is comparative. If motion pictures are to deflect from nature the face of virtue, they must also show the image of vice. To make virtue lovable and vice despicable, we must know what they are. We all admit there are decent and indecent, acceptable and unacceptable methods by which this ought to be done. Yet, it must be done or there can be no lessons from life; there can be no strengthening of character. By no system of wet-nursism can you solve the problem of delinquency or crime by hiding bad things or the truth about them, or by depriving children of the right, under proper conditions, to see, to hear and to know what they are.

They may be worse off if shielded from knowledge of evil or spared any contact with it. They will be better and stronger if wisely familiarized with evil in order to know how to avoid it—or, facing it, to conquer it. "Vice is a monster of such frightful mien, that to be hated needs but to be seen." And, of course, with equal truth there follows the warning as to what will happen if that truth is perverted. If youth are to learn to hate vice—to triumph over it rather than that it should triumph over them—we of the older generation must know how to wisely teach youth the truth about vice and crime.

We are losing sight in this country of some fundamental things about the whole problem of good and evil. As a result, when some of our reforms and crusades are won, we may be worse off than when we started. This was believed by many to be the case in the battle against booze. Prohibition was believed to be the best remedy. If some of our remedies do not fail altogether, they produce worse evils, or at least new evils. The kick that some people get out of reforming often blinds them to the facts about good and evil and how to overcome evil. A man on a jag is always blind to the things about him.

From all of my experience with literally thousands of delinquent youth I find it difficult to fairly and justly say that the cause of delinquency or crime was due just to what the offender had seen in the movies. Doubtless there are such cases. I think they are rarer than is generally supposed. I can be much more definite and certain in saying that I know of thousands of children who have positively been elevated, inspired and made happier because of the movies; who have been kept off the streets, out of alleys, the vulgar story telling of the barnyards, and a multitude of idle evil associations by the wholesome appeals, the family gatherings and educational opportunities afforded them by the movies. I really believe that if we had never had any motion pictures at all we would probably have more crime among youth than we now have, or at least we would have as much.

Nothing in the last fifty years of the most eventful history of all time has perhaps done more to reduce sin and crime and add to the happiness, education and progress of the human race than motion pictures, and if the right-minded intelligent people of this country will support the producers in giving us wholesome amusement they will certainly do more in this regard in the years to come.

The movies are going to do more than any other agency to prevent the greatest of all crimes, horrid war. Through motion pictures, all nations, peoples, races and creeds, all speaking the same language of the movies, are being brought into concord, acquaintanceship and understanding. And when they know and understand each other, they will love and cease to hate each other and war shall be no more. It is a real league of nations in binding them together through seeing that they are all just the same as each other—that there are no bad people and no good people when properly understood, but there are bad things and good things as they reflect through the bodies or behavior and conduct of people, depending on causes, which as yet we know little about, and that the great lesson of life is to learn how to wisely fight evil more and people less.

Mankind has conquered all the reptiles and the wild beasts that threatened his mastery of this planet. Why? Because, primarily, he could see them, because they were known to him. But he hasn't conquered all disease—that remains to threaten his dominion. And why? Because it is mostly the unseen beasts—the bugs, parasites and germs just now beginning to be seen. As with evil and disease, the movies will do more than all else besides to make them real—to make them known.

It is thus the greatest educator the world has ever had—the visual educator.

And when all things are seen and known to man, he becomes forever the undisputed sovereign of the world. Through visual education the average child of twelve is in the future to know more in academic education than the present college graduate. Largely through the movies, among the future great inventors of the world, we shall behold children from ten to twenty-one years of age.

How, O Master, shall we overcome evil—is still the eternal question of a war-ridden, hate-ridden, fearful world. Instead of any longer listening, it is growing listless to the eternal answer of the prophets—and "Overcome evil with good." He never said to overcome it through governmental suppression and the hate-breeding violence of forcible censorships. That was the answer of Pontius Pilate. And Pontius Pilate was the first great censor and Jesus Christ the first great victim of censorship. On behalf of this nation's childhood, whose destinies may be injured by such false remedies, I appeal from the gospel of Pilate to the gospel of Christ.

But what shall we do, you may ask, to guard that destiny which we all equally have at heart? It is not an easy thing always to know just how to overcome evil with good. It is much easier for some parents, teachers, unwise, if not ungracious pastors, to leave the job to a board of censors or some new-fangled statute law with its abuses, blackmails, grafts, persecutions, stupidities and tyrannies. Are we to be a nation of dodgers, of weazened shirkers, putting responsibility on laws, laws and more laws, bureaus, bureaucrats, censors and regulators until we are glutted, choked and suffocated with laws to let any George do it, but the right George?

Are we to become a nation of "squealers," passing the buck from parents, homes, schools and churches for their responsibility for Youth, to some perfectly human-to-err censors who may be wise and good but likely to be mostly foolish, if, as in the case of some of our former prohibition regulators, they are not crooks and grafters, to flounder to their own helplessness because they do not know what is good or what is evil or how to fight it.

Consider the fact that even now a picture that one governmental censor board says is good, another in some other state, condemns as bad. And consider the rank injustice of city or state censorship authorities passing a "bad" picture as "good" in one such city or state, and this same perfectly "good" picture as "bad" in another, as these different censorship boards often do.

Only gradually and painfully, through science mostly, now more and more the handmaiden of real education and real religion, shall we know how to overcome evil. It is always with good. It is too big a problem for me to give all my views here.

Now, I think a great deal of good could be done in the fight against evil if our parents and Sunday-school teachers would question youth more as to their motives for righteous conduct, and with more time and patience set them right as to their real meaning. You ask them why they do right and they will generally tell you that it is "to keep out of jail," or "the cop'll get me," or "I'd get a licking," or "I'll go to hell."

Thus, from perfectly well-intentioned teaching, what we are putting mostly in their lives is misunderstanding. That is, we are trying to get virtue too much by artificial restraints. These fears no longer serve as restraints and we are very much at fault in doing so little to sub-stitute natural restraints as these artificial ones are passing.

Fundamentally, it is our overstrain in the demand for these artificial restraints upon human conduct—restraints that come from without—that is making most of the delinquency among youth in this country. And their over-emphasis to the neglect of natural restraints is due perhaps more to ignorance in some of our institutions than the motion pictures. There is such a thing as going too far in our insatiate demand for these artificial re-straints. It is a greater crime against youth, fostered mostly by well-meaning people who are ignorant about youth. They are causing us to forget all about the more important restraints, or to indulge in a lazy indifference regarding them because of our mistaken faith in restraints so largely artificial.

As against these, what we need most in the lives of youth are the natural restraints. They come from within. They enable children and people, in the face of every evil and temptation, without being afraid to know about it, to see it or to hear about it, to be so fortified from within against it that they will stand up to meet it and conquer it. In other words, to have the strength of character to do right because it is right—not through the fear of punishment or the hope of rewards—but through true education and religion.

These artificial restraints, so long thus over-emphasized even in some well-meaning schools and churches, and beheld on every hand in demands for more suppressions, regulations, prohibitions, punishments, coercions and censorships, are failing. And it is our insistent refusal to substitute more of the natural restraints in homes, schools and churches, that is a real cause of delinquency in this country. You do not cure evil by more censorships and prohibitions, don'ts, *verbotens* and taboos. You are too often just adding fuel to the flame you are setting up in this country. The restraints of hell-fire and damnation are gone. They do not frighten any more. Those of policemen, prisons, and fears of punishments are of course still helpful in restraining certain types of weaklings and the vicious. The thing that makes most people good in this country is not these things. The thing that will make the bad ones good is more of the thing that has made the good ones good—the natural restraints.

I said good and evil are relative. You cannot helpfully know one without the other. They should, of course, appear in proper perspectives. Their relationship for moral uplift should be clear. I insist that the great majority of the movies do thus emphasize them in their true light. Vice is ever shown as the enemy and destroyer of human happiness; virtue as the only true course to secure the real joys of life; that achieves the only victories worth while.

In the movies, righteousness wins; sin loses. The hero triumphs. The villain bites the dust.

Not only decency but the pocketbook guarantees these general averages, and that general average is the best we can hope for in anything. Nothing is perfect. You cannot legislate right understanding into the human mind. By the more and more decent methods of showing life, as I believe to be more and more the rule in the movies, they furnish a great outlet, not only to the natural, wholesome craving for excitement and adventure, but for a necessary and legitimate amount of sex expression which otherwise, from sheer suppression, is far more harmful and more likely to result in sin and crime.

Some of the gossamer fabric of unreality, as in fantasies, dreams and fairy tales, is just as necessary in the movies as are the realities of life, to minister to the complexes and, as governors, to release the strange suppressions of nature. There is always to be expected the decent licenses of poetry and exaggerations of fiction.

It has become a national hobby of ours, in the absence of much good sense, to indulge in certain kinds of battles against evil that only makes us ridiculous. Each time, in each onslaught, we have some one thing for the "goat." Then we all assemble for the chase. For many of us it is great fun. For others, it is a grievous concern. At one time it is the legalized liquor traffic; at another, it is the cigarette or the automobile, the racy literature, the dance or jazz music. Each time it is this or that *one* thing that is causing all the sin. I do not know what it is going to be when the kids begin spooning in the clouds in the aerial autos of tomorrow. Neither the censors, nor the parents, nor the laws can follow them there. At the present time the "goat" is generally the movies.

No one deplores more than I do the commercialization of certain phases of what we call the sex appeal or improper crime stories in the movies. No one deplores more than I do some of the stupid, inartistic, vulgar, uncultural, silly things in the movies. They are there as in books or newspapers. If censorship were a practical remedy for anything, we might better have it against bad taste, bad manners and some of the stupid, boresome movies that can do no harm to anyone except waste their time, and because of their very insipid stupidity, would meet with the hearty approval of most any board of censors. It is all to be naturally expected in an industry or artistry so new. More patience, time and education are needed to correct them. No one is more anxious than I am to see them corrected. But it would be highly unjust not to, at the same time, keep in mind all that is right with the movies.

In their short life of scarcely a quarter of a century, they have done more to correct their follies and mistakes than literature and newspapers have done in a century.

When I deal with naughty children, I always find more good than evil in them, though their accusers seldom admit it. I get more out of them by praising them for the good they do than by condemning them for the evil they do. In this way do I succeed best. By working with them and not against them. Let us then, with this equally human thing, see all the wonderful improvement that has been made in recent years, not only artistically, from the standpoint of the producer, but also from that of the growing demand of the public for clean shows, and the splendid work of the producers in furnishing them.

And even when crime and vice are presented, when it must be done, more and more is it being done within the bounds of decency and with due regard to well-established rules that most every one knows and accepts. Few minds differ upon what is really obscenity and indecency. Nothing is being more frowned upon today than the stories written for a mere pornographic, sensual appeal, without any good purpose intended or accomplished. For all of such cases, we have the laws against obscenity and indecency which are not near as much used and enforced as they might be and could be.

And we ever have the appeal to public opinion. I believe it is in the end safe and sane in this country. And then there is being held out to us by the producers themselves the open door invitation to join hands with them to give the public the thing that it wants most and that is, clean, decent, wholesome pictures. The children are being provided with special films and opportunities to see them.

Co-operation between public and producer and exhibitor is being successfully accepted as one of the best methods of carrying on propaganda in this country for better, bigger and cleaner pictures.

The progress of art, science and literature in this country depends upon an unfettered, original creative imagination. There can be no progress or creative work anywhere with the hobble of censorship on these things at the helm. Freedom of thinkers, scientists, and artists does not mean degeneracy. It means justice, truth, progress, happiness, health and beauty. The chains of censorship mean irritation, reaction, bigotry, vice, immorality, gloom, degeneracy and death. Of course there are dangers in everything—

good and evil in everything—all dependent on its use and understanding. But I would a thousand times rather take my chances on too much freedom than too much of these artificial restraints.

In the regulation of human thought, as presented through instruction or entertainment in the motion pictures, books or newspapers, we have an entirely different problem. It is too dangerous to tamper with in any governmental, regulative, arbitrary way. To attempt it is to court the greater evils of bigotry and fanaticism, of racial, religious and class prejudices, of hatreds and tyrannies.

I would a thousand times rather see civilization subjected to all the dangers which may lurk in an entirely unregulated and uncensored press, or of books, plays or motion pictures, than to risk the far greater evils of arbitrary, forcible, governmental censorship regulation.

There are no committees of people on earth who have any such super-wisdom or right to exercise any such power, no matter how commendable its purpose may be.

Those who propose such remedies for youthful delinquencies are honest but mistaken. I wish they could all be convinced. I know their purposes are good. I wish they would join the multitude of constructive fathers, mothers, preachers, teachers, business men and citizens, through the work of the home, school, church and press, enlisting, as I believe we can, co-operation and help of those who produce and distribute the movies themselves, to get bigger, better and cleaner pictures.

Decorating the walls of many a school room, we have held up to us a picture of the gallant youth St. George, in pursuit of the Dragon. It is an interesting poster. It has for us a great lesson. But I sometimes wonder if it is understood. In this picture, St. George is clad in armor.

It is the symbol of HIS OWN STRENGTH and power to meet and slay the dragon—the evil he encounters.

Thus, down the path of life you have him started. He goes alone. He is protected by no governmental wet-nursism. No censors have preceded him to chase the dragons from his path. Now, just imagine the censors doing that, be they a certain type of "dear-old ladies" of both sexes who never will be satisfied that anything is good if it pictures vice or crime, or well-meaning Puritans with worse complexes, or crafty politicians with itching palms, snooping into every crack and cranny for the smell of dragons (evil) to shoo them off the path before young George may proceed upon his way.

I hear them saying, "Come on, Georgie, dear boy; the path is clear; we censors have done your work; we have seen to it that not even a suspicious tabby cat can cross your path. You have no fight to make; we will spare you even the sight of a dragon (evil) on the road."

Is that what you are going to do to Young America? Change the noble knighthood of conflict and struggle to the milksophood of apron strings? Yet such is governmental censorship. Against it, I protest. Against it, modern youth revolts. In their name, we must avoid a step so fatal and so false.

We do not want to make mollycoddles of this younger generation because a few morons or even alert, but vicious-minded persons have become criminals from something good or bad they have seen in the movies. We do not want to see methods adopted in mistaken purpose of fighting evil whose effect is only to make insipid, dependent, hot-house plants of modern youth.

We want to see a self-reliant Young America. We want to see it grow to sturdy manhood, like the oak that faces and fights the storm and fights best where the foe is known best and encountered most. Prepare Youth for the Path.

This is the only right way to successfully equip the youth of America with moral, physical and mental efficiency. Then, and only then, as modern St. Georges, thus armored, they can be trusted THEMSELVES to meet the dragons of evil that cross the path of life. For down that path they have to go. You cannot prepare the path for them.

It is our job to prepare youth for the path, the big job parents, teachers and preachers are neglecting in their mistaken effort too much to prepare the path for them. There must be more preparing youth for the path and less preparing the path for youth. Then with perfect faith, you can trust him to go down that path, and though it be strewn with dragon's teeth, he will emerge triumphant, the glorious youth that he is—Young America, the noblest, bravest, wisest, most loyal, generous and just that the world has ever seen.

CHAPTER VI

THE MOVIES AND THE FARM PEOPLE

by

BENJAMIN HORACE HIBBARD

THE question may very properly be asked why there should be a discussion of farmers and the movies, any more than there should be a discussion of merchants and the movies, or weavers and the movies. There may be good reasons for discussing these other classes in their relations to the movies, and there may not, since these people live in aggregations of considerable numbers, and usually commingled with other occupational groups into societies of such complexity that as separate entities they do not exist at all. On the contrary the farmers live apart from all other occupational groups; they have traits of their own. Having lived a somewhat more isolated life they are distinctly more individualistic, more rigid in their moral conceptions, more orthodox in religion. These characteristics are said to be vanishing, and the view is often expressed that farmers are just like other people. No doubt the peculiar characteristics of farmers are vanishing, but just how rapidly is quite another question. They most distinctly have not by any means all vanished yet, nor will they within a generation. Fundamental characteristics do not change as readily as haircuts, styles of clothes, means of locomotion, or facilities for entertainment. The

64

farmer's character is moulded largely by the circumstances of his home and his work. He lives and works in the main apart from others. Normally, farmers work in the daytime and stay home evenings. It is not, therefore, surprising that as movie prospects they promise less, and pay less, to the movie operator than is to be expected from any other quarter of our people.

It is reported that about a third of the American people attend the movies at least to some extent. No satisfactory survey has yet been made showing exactly who the movie-going groups are. There are, however, sufficient facts available to show unmistakably that city people furnish the bulk of the patronage. It is reported on good authority that the city young people who go to movies attend about once a week. In one mid-western county a careful survey showed that the attendants from the farm districts went about once a month. While not too much dependence may be put on these proportions in the way of final accuracy, they are undoubtedly quite representative of the general facts. Movie attendance in proportion to population is outstandingly urban.

The explanation of the fact that city people go to the movies much more than do country people is not at all difficult in the main, though it may not be possible to present a full and complete list and analysis of the causes. Probably first comes the fact that city people are conveniently located, that is to say, handy to the movie theatres, as compared with the country people as a whole. Next, and almost as important, come two additional and closely related considerations controlling spending. The people of the city have more current cash in their pockets, and a more highly developed habit of spending. Farmers have, as a class, a definite economic goal toward which they are struggling. A similar ideal is not only prevalent in the city, but within a comparatively narrow circle is more highly developed and more dominant. The majority of city people are not so definitely and specifically motivated. They own little or no property, have a fairly good income, and indulge themselves much more generously. It is not at all hard to understand why city people are the mainstay of the movies. They are the mainstay of the theatre in general, of sports, and all manner of commercialized entertainment, amusement, and culture.

The country has from time immemorial furnished the bulk of its own entertainment. It has had its spelling schools, singing schools, debating societies, dances, baseball, picnics, and donation parties. Probably from one very important standpoint the country type of entertainment has differed from the city type in that the city people have for many years hired an entertainer to put on a show for them while the country people have entertained themselves by putting on their own shows. Much can be said in favor of active as compared with passive entertainment. The country people probably do not consciously stay away from the pointless and vitiating movie in order to develop their wits in playing bridge, nor do the young people refrain from going to movies in order to spend more time and energy in improving their skill in spelling, in developing accuracy in eye and hand in playing amateur baseball, nor yet in developing social graces at a barn dance or husking bee. Nevertheless, the movie has a somewhat weaker appeal among people who can to a considerable degree stage their own amusements than among those who have traditionally paid some one else to entertain them. And finally it will, and must, be admitted that sparseness of population in the country district is the greatest factor providing a measure of immunity of country people to the movies.

Another undoubted base of resistance of country people to the movies, varying from a full hundred per cent down to nothing at all from group to group, perhaps one might almost say from the most to the least sophisticated, is the moral slant or conviction. In the main the country is more conservative than the city, and just as the country voter is less trouble to the party candidate than is the city voter, so also religion and moral convictions undergo less frequent revisions and overhaulings in the country than in the city. Religious taboos fare better in the vicinities in which life is less disturbed and torn by the changes of industrialism, the styles of fashion, and the surge of untried nostrums and isms. These conditions obtain in the country. Hence the morality of the country, as compared to that of the city, may not be higher or better, but it is more securely anchored to the past, to that which has the approval of the older and accepted moralists. One is not surprised to learn that one of the great Protestant churches kept in its discipline for years clauses forbidding its members to indulge in certain forms of amusements in spite of the fact that its city contingent was paying no attention to the ban. The country delegates were strong enough for a generation or two to keep the liberals from breaking down the supposed safeguards.

Are then the farm people opposed to the movies? No,

not as a whole, and probably not in general. They are, however, distinctly opposed, and most properly so, to a large part of the movies which have been presented to the public during the past fifteen years. Do they fail to attend mainly because of moral objections? There is little information on this point. That there are other good and undoubted explanations of the small attendance of country people at the movies has been admitted, but the morality phase of the case must not be overlooked. It was no accident that the calumniator of Darwin staged his last great stand within the fastnesses of the southeastern mountains. There is an unworked field for the movies among country people, and the producer who aspires to occupy this field must understand their moral fiber and religious convictions.

A question which every movie exhibitor must ask himself is: What will take with my patrons? In every village, of three thousand or less, the patronage comes as much from the farms as from the village. Under such circumstances it is no idle question as to the tastes of the farm people. Will they come to see the "Grand Hotel," or the "Red-Headed Woman"? Of course there is no movie which will attract, or repel, all people of any considerable class. However, it is pretty generally admitted that farm people do not care for the off-color films. Neither do the self-respecting people of the village care for these shows. If for no better reason they do not, in a small community, where everybody knows what everybody else does, care to be seen going in through the front door of the little village show house while "Possessed" is blazoned forth on the billboards. The farmers have the same feeling with probably a still stronger conviction that the road to such scenes is the road to hell.

How about the country people and the plays based on the good stories, new or old? Will "David Copperfield" take in village and farm community? Will "Little Women," "Alice in Wonderland" or George Arliss in "Richelieu" bring in the people from the small centers and the sparsely settled countryside? At least not equally well. In the small place a film like "Little Women" will go moderately well; not the best by any means. Nothing like all our people know Louisa M. Alcott and her writings well enough to be drawn to a play which involves no stirring love story, has no display of physical prowess, and nothing very closely associated with the active life of farming. But are not the scenes from home life of universal appeal? Perhaps, but the appeal is many times stronger in those who have had the experiences of living those scenes over with Miss Alcott, through the pages of the book, than to those who know little or nothing about the story in advance of the presentation by the talkie. It is an event in the lives of those who have known Jo and Beth and Amy as story characters to meet them, as it were, face to face, hear their voices, and find that they are just as human as any of us. As to "David Copperfield" there is much doubt in the minds of many country film exhibitors. One of them recently said, "No, I don't want 'David Copperfield.' Of course there are probably enough people in my town who know enough about the book on which it is based, or enough about Dickens in general, to fill the house a time or two, but what about the other two or three days? Give me a Zane Grey story if you please, and I'll fill up the house for half a week." The only reason the country town exhibitor is not enthusiastic about "Alice in Wonderland" is because there are too few children in his community. They don't fill the house, or at least not many times. In a city it takes at least moderately well. The country people praise it, but they don't make it pay.

Well then, how about "Richelieu"? There are too few of us who know much about him, and it is no criticism of the farmers to say that to very few of them is "Richelieu" a real character. All people like to see and hear things which they know at least something about. Farmers are no different from any one else in this respect. They like the western movies because of the riding, which is thrilling to a wide range of people, but more especially so to farm people because of their intimate acquaintance with the horse. It is therefore nothing strange that at the small town theatre Tom Mix and Buck Jones continue to draw good houses. Everyone, young and old, on the farm has ridden a horse, and every young man, and many others, have profound respect for the skilful and daring rider. A cattle round-up, or a stampede, will make the nerves of every farm youth tingle. They know more about what it means than does a dry-goods clerk.

Another line of acting which appeals to the country people, less hardened to the triumph of the wicked than many an urbanite, is the play in which the villain after many narrow escapes, is finally trapped and taken in hand by the bluff, burly sheriff "who always gets his man." Then it must not be overlooked that people like to see themselves, in the composite, depicted on the stage. Not a caricature, but a real, honest presentation is what they

want. Thus the "County Chairman" with Will Rogers
is a grand success. To begin with it helps greatly for all
audiences to meet in the movies the characters which
they have got acquainted with over the radio, and through
the press. Will Rogers had friends and admirers in every
country in the Union, and is appreciated just as keenly in
the farming districts as anywhere. Every one who has lived
among the open fields can see "David Harum," or the
"County Chairman," very vividly in the memories of old
neighbors, or possibly something very like them in characters of the day. Showing people to themselves has been
the highest art of the playwright and the player, from
Shakespeare and Sheridan, to Maud Adams and Marie
Dressler. But, someone will very properly ask, do not
the producers know all of these points even better than
the layman? In a sense, yes. The producers, however, are
interested in big stakes. Their main income has been the
city patronage, with the country patronage an adjunct.
Through "block booking" the country trade has been
obliged to take the same films that are shown in the city.
Part of them fit well, part very badly.

Manifestly the movie producers have never taken the
farmers into account. They have had such a rich and constant harvest in the city where wealth abounds, and where
small sums are not missed, or at least not pinched or
prized, that the outlying regions where loose change is
neither so abundant nor so free has not attracted attention
either as furnishing a setting for some of the scenes or as
a place for the sale of admission tickets. On the other
hand, it would seem that warnings against the rottenness
of the films have impressed more deeply the country than

the city parents and preachers. If the inference be correct, it remains for some enterprising and clever producer to stage a few films of special appeal to the country people. If these people have resisted the allurements and wiles of the films of the past decade and a half there should by all means be left among us an unspoiled remnant, not surfeited and disgusted with the mire and filth through which the movie-going world has been trailed year after year. For except the lords of Hollywood had left us this very small remnant, we should have been more hopelessly bankrupt in the way of delicacy and decency required of our movies than we are. The long list of movies of questionable moral tone, and the equally sorry list of unquestionable immoral tone held the stage for a long decade, and to what extent the conversion to better citizenship and decency is genuine and lasting is open to debate. However, there is a most gratifying appearance among the movies of today of a distinctly high type of production. Even so, snobbery, drinking, shooting, crime, intriguing, sex, divorce, and deceit still predominate in the majority of pictures.

The producers have frequently resorted to sophistry in defending themselves against criticisms. They have insisted that they were endeavoring to depict life. That what people wanted was realism, and that their pictures were such. They have even claimed that crime, and more especially gross immorality, marital infidelity, flippancy, and the whole trail of debauchery, over which we, and especially our children, have been dragged, is after all real life and must not be ignored or glossed over.

We ask almost aghast whether or not these lurid scenes

depict real life. Unquestionably they do. But is it all, or a fair sample, of real life? The characters of "Main Street" are perhaps real enough, but the whole story is not. Any self-respecting citizen of the small town might safely defy Sinclair Lewis to show one single sample of country town, three thousand in size, in which all human beings, almost without exception, are sordid, selfish, brutal, and petty. There is no such town. But aren't they, his characters, in themselves, true to life? Yes, but they proclaim in loud tones a gigantic untruth. If one should go to the best kept city with a high priced, high powered, camera and photograph all the back doors, garbage cans, dirty children, and mongrel dogs, and publish them under the title: "True Views of X," they would be, at one and the same time, metriculously truthful, and slanderously false. Just so snobbery and villainy represent real life, but only a fraction of it, and thus, as depicted, they come far short of telling the truth. In defense of those responsible for so presenting them it may be said that they were never designed to do so.

The last stage of insult comes in the moralizing of the perpetrators: These sordid scenes teach resistance to evil; inculcate lessons of mastery over circumstances; self control. We must face the stern fact that the age of childish innocence is past! Of course the real explanation of all this is so simple that polysyllables, and circumlocution are quite uncalled for. It is wholly and clearly a matter of box office receipts, no more, no less. The producers are missionaries of their banker backers. The actors are not asked to pass upon the desirability or the manner of presenting the scenes. The producers may have been

during the past in collusion among themselves to prove
that every man has his price, or to disprove the old copy-
book precept that "Vice is a monster of such frightful
mien—." Or again they may have felt that the Philip-
pians were ill-advised respecting "whatsoever things are
pure, whatsoever things are lovely, whatsoever things are
of good report." The things unlovely and of bad report
have appeared to swell the salary rolls and bank accounts,
and it must be admitted, while listening to the movies,
that money talks, both on, and back of, the screen.

The recent financial distress of the movie business and
the appearance of a considerable number of commendable
films may not be unrelated. Not that all the older films
were without merit. Many of them have been wonderful,
and far above reproach, but along with the good we
have had an overweight of dung. The producers abandoned the films of the "Flaming Youth" and "Damaged
Goods" order much after the manner in which Henry
Ford abandoned the "Model T."—after the public refused
to buy. The trouble with the salacious film is that it lacks
the power of growth. When once a generation of movie
goers has had its fill of filth there isn't much more for
the producers to do. Now without letting go of the old
charms they are reaching out for a better measure of
wholesome productions. It is no doubt gratifying to
know, or at least to believe, that the public is positively
demanding these changes, rather than that a conversion
has occurred primarily in Hollywood. If the former
proves to be the case it will be more lasting, and more
positive. We have, of course, become familiar with the
lip service of the moral czar of moviedom: Things are

getting better. The movie producers are sensitive to moral demands. They are determined to give the public pictures which will appeal to the whole family, and be approved by the ministers. Following which declarations they issue various statements to the public pledging their hearts and hands to a better, cleaner, and more cultured type of movie. The latest of such is the "Code." Here the movie producers pledge themselves, or at least agree to "maintain right moral standards." And why not since they are the judges of what is right? However, some of the producers are hopeful that the ultimate outcome of movie influence on mankind may be signal, sweeping, and salutary. One of the leading producers writing in a popular magazine under the title, "The Public Is Always Right," closes with the noble, assuring statement that "we who are in the making of the films must take the great trust seriously." [1] They always have. It is the motivating force back of the seriousness which we deplore. Anyhow the great producers are not in favor of censorship: "And there has been much talk of censorship. We have had some of it and the great natural power of the movies has been almost throttled by it." But there are cases in which censorship has increased the "gross." The climax of the article from which these sentences are quoted comes at the close: "The movie and the radio will bring people together. They will make for unity and a certain great oneness of the world. Ultimately it may even be oneness with God." A twelfth of a century has passed since these reverent words were penned. The "oneness" still seems, so far as the output of the first of

[1] Ladies Home Journal. September 1927.

these great unifying forces is concerned, to be leading to God via the bathroom and bedroom route.

Undoubtedly the movies will improve; undoubtedly there will be, of necessity, a catering to the desires and demands of the public. Just as undoubtedly there will be a persistence which only greed can furnish to perpetuate the undesirable because it has, in the past, paid. The average chronic movie-goer takes the bad with the good and no one knows to a nicety just what pleases him best. That he likes a good deal of what most boards of censorship would reject is too true. That an equal patronage would, in the long run, be accorded a higher type of production is more than possible, but those who are responsible for the plans and specifications of any structure are not easily persuaded that anything else would do as well. To make the change is to create a new problem and new hazards.

Since transition periods are critical and since these are trying times for movies, it would seem that the occasion was at hand for taking stock anew respecting the demands of the farm, and village people, who must be grouped together in this interest. It appears to be true that these people do not approve as fully as do those of the city of the movies which have to date predominated. From the exploitation standpoint there are still in the country districts millions of potential movie-goers who go seldom or never. Certainly this market is not to be permanently ignored. It will be captured by some producer who comprehends the undoubted fact that just as tastes differ from group to group regarding clothes, food, drink, sermons and marriage, so also the tastes of country and city are unlike regarding the theatre whether in the "legitimate" form or in the movies. The country has accepted the movie as it is largely because of the dearth of choice.

From the standpoint of a more wholesome movie, two hopeful and positive influences have recently come into action. First came the "Payne Fund," through the use of which many painstaking, convincing studies have been made, on the influence of the movie and the radio on the youth of the country. The findings, in some instances, will of course be questioned, and challenged. No criticisms will, however, be able to wipe out the influence of the convincing findings of the many research workers who have made the studies. They appear to be irrefutable, even though not in every sense adequate and finished.

The other influence, fully as hopeful, is an attack on the demand side of the movie business,—the Legion of Decency, more recently launched by the Catholics. There will be a great deal of support for this movement not alone among Catholics, but likewise among Protestants. If the Catholics, the leaders of the movement, show the energy and finesse for which they have long been known, there is likely to be a rather prompt change of heart and judgment on the part of the producers and distributors of film pictures, for after all, "The Public Is Always Right." The most vital consideration is, who leads the public in its thinking? The Legion of Decency is bound to have a powerful following in the country districts. If this comes to pass it will be the immediate task of the producers to discover, without delay, what the needs and tastes of a large contingency of our people are, and these clever and shrewd directors of productions, of public thought and morals, are capable of the necessary adjustments. With the facts and judgment furnished by the research workers now available, and the determined campaign of a powerful organization bent on reforming a leading institution of recreation, education, and culture, a gleam of light should be visible through the drab setting of the movie morals.

CHAPTER VII

THE MOVIES AND THE FAMILY

by

JONAH J. GOLDSTEIN

WHEN I use the word "family" in this chapter, I have reference to the average American family—such as we find in the lower-earning brackets. The wealthy (a very small percentage of our population) manage to provide for themselves a sufficient variety of entertainment.

Judged from the social standpoint, the entertainment film can render no greater service than wholesome recreation to the masses. Because of the physical condition in the slum districts of our cities, the home is too often not the place to go to, but rather a place to keep away from. The tenement dweller returns home chiefly to sleep. If he stays around the house, it is because he cannot afford to go to places of amusement. In the crowded spaces of our tenements, youngsters, particularly in large families, are in the way. Because of insufficient recreation and play spaces, they are compelled to play in the streets —and the gutter is the most prominent part of the street. The problem of entertainment also affects our rural families; and films are easily available and economical.

There is no more welcome beacon to the poor man's family than the blinking lights of the movie house which can furnish worthwhile recreation. Film houses are important in a community because they have the power to lessen discontent and delinquency. They relieve the drabness of an idle leisure that makes men and women despondent, disgruntled and defiant. If private industry did not supply such recreational facilities, the state probably would have to. Wholesome recreation is not a venture in state philanthrophy; it is a form of social insurance against disorder and crime.

There has been much protest recently by religious and educational groups against the type of film that has been offered for public consumption.

The point of clash is fundamentally simple. The movie producer builds his program on a basis of entertainment value as reflected by box-office receipts—paying too little attention to anything else. The movies have their aftermath. Some of the results are purely physical reactions; many a young woman, for example, picks her new dress on the basis of what the leading lady wore. Harder to evaluate, but just as definitely present, are certain ethical and spiritual concepts that influence the audience.

Church and educational authorities which have for their primary function the protection and nurturing of the family and its members have criticized the type of pictures produced. This group is best in a position to appreciate the reactions of the family, but in its energetic battle, it sometimes forgets that on the whole, motion pictures are essentially for entertainment—a most important part of a community program, particularly in times of economic distress. (There are some of us who use the movies as a "whipping boy" to explain all that is evil, in order to cover up weakness in the performance of their own educational work.) Moreover, the screen, by reason of its availability and inchoate versatility is bound to play an important part in the new leisure which must be the inevitable result of the lessening of hours spent daily in gaining a livelihood.

The problem is not one of compromise or conciliation. Movie producers justified their productions by declaring, "we are giving the people what they want." Church and school denied this.

Large bodies move slowly; but the laws of inertia are inexorable. The tremendous community of American families tolerated whatever was thrust at them by the moving picture houses all over the country, just so long. Then the American Family rose in its might and delivered the blow where it hurt most—at the ticket window. Offending members of the industry found that by and large, this country is composed of clean-living and clean-thinking citizens; and they further found that there is a definite financial penalty for failing to produce attractions that cater to clean-living and clean-thinking citizens. A demonstration of the kind so recently staged makes that patent; what is just as important, it demonstrates that an aroused public opinion still asserts its dominance.

I have frequently had occasion to say that the wearing of the judicial gown endows no man with omniscience; nevertheless, years on the bench do train one to view controversies objectively, with an eye to both sides— which doesn't mean straddle.

Every business and profession has its extremists; and I no more agree with those of the motion-picture profession who feel that the industry is perfect, than I do with those who take the attitude that the industry has replaced money as the root of all evil.

The influence of the motion pictures in moulding thought was again brought home to me when I recently assisted in an experiment at the University Settlement in New York City, by which a typical group of boys averaging thirteen years of age was shown the inner mechanism of various governmental agencies which they had never before seen in real life. After several hours in a court-room, they were invited to ask questions. The result is uninteresting if we merely note that more than half the questions were based on comparisons to "the way it happens in the movies"; it is uninteresting because this was to be expected on the basis of the many experiments that have been conducted along these lines. But very interesting, when we consider that these children spent twenty-five hours a week in school and averaged no more than three hours a week at the cinema. And even more interesting when we remember that these questions were along lines not given much attention by the educational authorities. The lads were very acute at observation and were able to apply their own knowledge to what they observed.

These boys were on the whole not different from their parents and families. Many of the parents would have shared the wonderment of the lad who expressed the viewpoint of the group when he said: "Gee, the detectives ain't dumb like they are in the movies!"

Nevertheless, no reasonable person can say that the movies are the inspiration of all evil in the community any more than one can say that every right-thinking citizen is a direct result of the copy-book maxims which are taught through school. As a matter of fact, because of compulsory education, the majority of our criminals studied exactly the same maxims as our examplary citizens.

Of course, there are standards that must be met. These however, are fixed by time, place, geography and all the elements that make for a constantly changing world.

The appeal of the many good films now showing is in their manner of telling the favorite stories of literature. Recently, worthwhile productions have attracted many who formerly remained away.

There is more than mere box-office significance in the huge success of "Mickey Mouse" cavorting on the screen. Judged by the standards of family appeal, it is the greatest single entertainment feature ever produced by the motion-picture industry. Kings, philosophers, august statesmen, and little children have paid "Mickey Mouse" the honest tribute of unrestrained laughter, just as wise men and children in our times and before us have found recreation and intellectual content in reading "Alice in Wonderland."

There can be no doubt that the entertainment value is the main function of the motion-picture industry.

Education is planned and controlled by the few—movies are controlled by the sentiments of the many.

Sometimes in carrying out the duties with which they are charged, our teachers and clergy forget some of the fundamental principles of pedagogy. We learn, often, by example; but if properly presented we can often learn more from what might be termed an unfortunate situation than a good example. From a practical standpoint, showing the eight-year-old all the nice boys who don't play with matches is not merely as effective as showing him the lad who is wearing bandages because he played with fire.

The adults in the family should make it their business to interpret for the youngsters what they have seen at the movies. This will have a double effect, for at the same time it will cause them to draw their own moral lessons, which they may be inclined to ignore while exploring the entertainment possibilities of human-interest situations which lend themselves to ready and graphic exploitation by authors and producers. This is not to be interpreted as an argument for or in defense of the salacious, but in these times of early maturity for youngsters, it is ridiculous to think that they are in ignorance of what so often are facetiously called "the facts of life." It is much more important to realize what the state of education is, so that instead of permitting the youngster to draw conclusions which frequently are as incorrect as they are unhealthy, he may be guided to a proper sense of proportion for his later years. This is a sound principle for any moral, spiritual or ethical problem.

Such an approach would at least have the beneficent effect of giving the family a common meeting-ground for diversion and discussion. Not that every picture would or could have universal appeal for every member of the family; that is not demanded of any type of entertainment. It would be just as ridiculous to suggest that every book of fiction should be equally enjoyed by all members of the same household. Yet, there are enough pictures made so that by home education in that type, the child would become accustomed to evaluating what he sees.

I hasten to add that this suggestion is not offered as a panacea; it would merely help in the solution of a problem. After all, we have not as yet arrived at the stage where it can be predicted exactly what effect certain pictures will have on different individuals. This is as true for the adult as it is for the youngsters.

Professor Raymond Moley whose thoughts and utterances are always worthy of most serious attention said:

"I spent a good many years in the study of crime and criminal justice, and of necessity was compelled to examine with a considerable amount of care the entire question of crime, its causes and its results.

"In the first place, there is very, very great difference of opinion even among the so-called experts of the subject as to the effect of motion pictures upon crime. My judgment on this is based on an examination of most of what has been written on it, although I do say that psychologists have never given us anything approaching a reliable guide on the subject.

"Studies are made of motion pictures, in which children are asked where they got this idea or that. Then these answers are compiled, and an indictment of the motion pictures is made.

"I am sorry that other obligations and duties have prevented me from writing what I conceive might be a satirical piece of literature. One could go to any Sunday School and ask the boys whether they had ever been to Sunday School after having been to a movie, and the answer would be the same, because presumably they have been to a lot of movies in their lives. In one case they have gone to Sunday School, and in the other case they committed a crime. It just does not mean anything. The thing can be reduced to the greatest absurdity.

"All of the pseudo-scientific research which, I believe, should be very carefully examined before those leaders of opinion who do the talking in the world accept it as authentically scientific."

Seeing the problem clearly, the answer is not too difficult. Church and school must remember that their function is to educate and guide the family, and that, incidentally, such education and guidance is the quickest and surest means of raising the standards of the great mass; if they continue to attend to their primary functions, moving pictures will get better by force of public opinion.

The motion-picture industry so long as it remains an entertainment value must do nothing to interfere with the functions of those concerned with the family, and must co-operate wherever possible by choosing its material carefully and executing artistically.

Each group must understand the function of the other, and the mutual understanding can be the basis of a partnership that will lead to better family life. Equally important, the good will of the family will pay the dividends so necessary to every industry.

CHAPTER VIII

THE STORY IS THE THING

by

DON MARQUIS

THE moving pictures coming out of Hollywood actually are getting better, on the whole. There is a greater proportion of positively good pictures, outstanding achievements. And the quality of the run-of-the-mill product is, on the whole, a little better than it was a few years ago.

This improvement is due to the fact that the responsible executives are at last waking up to the fact that the moving picture has just one thing to peddle to the public —Story. Both the artistic quality of the product and the business success of the industry depend on the studios having somebody preside over each picture who thoroughly understands the element of Story.

A moving picture is necessarily a work of co-operation and collaboration. The creative element and the technical element must get together and function as one. There must be a blending of the imagination and the physical mechanism which objectifies its visions. This collaboration must be guided and bossed by some one who is as thoroughly aware of Story values as the man or men who write the script.

Hollywood is not wanting in people who understand

what constitutes Story—neither in writers, nor in directors, nor in competent actors.

Why is it, then, that so many inferior screen plays have been turned out by these competent men?

One trouble has been in a defect of organization. Wherever an executive in direct charge of production knows Story importance and values, he has been able to get a good screen play. But in too many instances production authority has been delegated to a number of second-string executives who don't know their business. They did not themselves have a definite idea of Story values, and the result was a series of fuzzy conferences in which the picture in the process of making started wrong, went further, and fared worse. A good many of these subordinate executives had their important jobs for any other reason except their ability or special fitness for the work —through some species of favoritism, possibly relationship to important people, close friendship, or some similar cause. They had to do something to justify their existence. They had to act busy about something. Therefore they interfered and hampered the work of directors and authors who really knew their business.

Indecision and incompetence on the part of an executive in charge of production (no matter what his title may be) results in a sloppily made story, which is also an expensively made story.

Sloppily made, because it lacks the control of one guiding mind—of one person who knows his business— or of several persons in collaboration who are competent and know what they are aiming for so definitely that their minds constitute practically one guiding mind.

The uncertainty, indecision and false starts, which result from the person in direct charge of production not knowing what constitute Story, make the process of filming a screen show a lengthy, confused process. And this runs into overhead expense, what with salaries, story costs, and this and that, which is considerable.

A man in charge of a picture who has not from the start a definite, clean-cut notion of the story he is trying to make, will vacillate and hesitate, and waste time and money. He will be experimental in his methods; he will shoot thousands of feet of film which will not do. This results in numerous re-takes and practically a complete reconstruction of the screen play while it is in the process of manufacture. That sort of thing can run into big money. The equipment is on the location, the actors, directors, camera men, electricians, writers, technical people of all sorts, are under salary, while the executive is changing and re-changing his mind. The cost of the wasted film itself is not a small matter.

A great part of this waste is prevented, and both the artistic end and the business end benefit—the expenditure being kept down to a reasonable figure—when the man in charge of production knows from the inception of the play exactly what he wants to do. He must be a creative artist himself. Not only for the sake of producing an artistic picture, but also for the sake of holding down expenses.

When the man in charge of a picture is not an artist —when he doesn't know Story—and know how to get it by an economy of creative effort, which in this business is also an economy of money—his picture will cost so

much to make that it will have to gross anywhere from
a third of a million to a million dollars at the box offices
in order to break even or show a profit.

This means that it must have a very wide audience;
an audience of many millions. Here enters a vicious
circle. The picture must be "sure-fire" stuff. It can't be
"high-brow." What, therefore, shall its appeal be based
on? In innumerable cases its appeal has been based on
sex and crime. Those elements in a picture appeal to
millions.

There is a very large audience which responds to a more
intellectual appeal. It is large enough to respond to a
better class of picture than it has been getting until
recently, in numbers which make the better-class picture
profitable. A more liberal use of brains and organizing
ability would turn out pictures that would please this
considerable element, and they would not have to gross
millions at the box offices to be profitable, since the brains
and organization cut down the production expense. It
is the picture compounded of gilded trash which costs
the most money and has to bring in the most money. The
real prosperity of the business, in the long run, depends
on cutting down on the junk and giving this large public
pretty good stuff, produced at a reasonable price and sold
at a reasonable profit.

It is the wasteful method of production which compels
the moving pictures to seek the prodigiously large audiences. The average mental level of this audience re-acts
upon the producers in turn—and they are apt to think of
it as being dumber than it really is, at that—and they have
been too apt to be afraid of letting what imagination is

available to them find its outlet in the films. They are afraid to produce and exploit anything which has not been proved acceptable to the wide audience of childish minds or trashy minds; and the childish mind is easily made into a trashy mind.

The improvement of the pictures in a moral way cannot be separated from the improvement of the pictures in an artistic and business way, for the three things stem from the same root; and the answer is that artistic quality has its effect upon moral content, educating the bad taste which debases moral content.

The question of a moral censorship is a very ticklish one. If such a thing as a general legal censorship is clamped down upon the pictures, the inevitable result must be the exclusion of many good pictures and artistic pictures which contain a moral lesson and enforce this lesson by an exhibition of abuses. With a censorship, all the elements interested in the perpetuation of these abuses will inevitably prevail upon the censorship to abolish the pictures exposing the abuses, under the guise of protecting the public mind from indecency. This happens in regard to books and the stage whenever a censorship is attempted. The only censorship needed is the encouragement of good taste artistically in the manufacture of films, and this through its artistic quality will inevitably take care of the question of any indecency in the pictures. This works back once again to the matter of artistic control and to placing the executive control of production in the hands of those who understand what Story is.

CHAPTER IX

STORIES I'D LIKE TO SEE SCREENED

by

WILLIAM LYON PHELPS

YEARS ago, when many church members thought it
either wicked or inconsistent with their profession to
enter a playhouse, a student in the classroom at the Yale
Divinity School asked Professor George Fisher: "Is it
right to go to the theatre?" The Professor replied by
asking, *"What* theatre?"

In those days thousands asked that question and
thousands answered in the negative. But such a question
and such an answer lacked intelligence. It might be
wrong to attend and thus support some theatrical productions, but it was wrong not to attend certain others.
It is a sin to neglect good opportunities, as it is more
virtuous to do good than merely to shun evil.

The legitimate theatre now being confined mainly to
New York and to a few traveling companies, the only
universal form of drama is the motion picture. The
movies are in every city and at nearly every crossroad;
they are the most popular form of theatrical entertainment the world has ever known. It is therefore not surprising that the nature of their influence is one of the
burning questions of the day; not to be answered off-
hand, and not to be dismissed with indifference.

The improvements made in inventions are as astounding as the invention itself. The first motion picture I saw in the kinetoscope; I peeped through a slit and saw moving, microscopic figurines. How could I, at the time, have foreseen such a magnificent talkie as "The Invisible Man?"

There are good movies and bad movies, just as there are the best and the worst opportunities in Paris. The good or bad effect of the movies depends on the use people make of them. At this moment the movies are under fire; they are being attacked for indecency, immorality, as inciters to crime, as panders to lust. Myself, I cannot remember ever having seen a movie that was immoral, except once; that was a very brief one, and it came as a part of a long and varied program in a foreign city.

I suppose many movies are immoral, because otherwise the assault against them would not be so widespread and so specific. The advertisements of movies, either in the newspapers or at the portals of the theatre, usually give them away; apparently some appeal to lust and some to idiocy; I do not care to waste time or money on such drivel.

However strong the attack on the impropriety of certain pictures may be, the screen has survived a more dangerous attack and survived by merit. Only a few years ago, there were many intelligent critics who condemned the movies altogether; they regarded them as inane, stupid, crude, idiotic. Furthermore, many respectable persons said with a rather superior air: "I never go to the movies." One hears comparatively little of such sweeping condemnation today; because the art of the movies has developed so amazingly that to ignore them would be a serious error. One would miss something important in modern civilization.

There are plenty of movies that are not only good, but superb; not only interesting, but thrilling; not only instructive, but inspiring; not only amusing, but side-splitting. And helpless, uncontrollable, roaring laughter is good for everybody.

The movie is like the radio. If a visitor from another planet tuned in on a certain evening and heard some features on the radio, he would think the population of the earth was composed of idiots; but suppose he tuned in on Walter Damrosch, or a great symphony orchestra, or on Harry Emerson Fosdick? Then he might over-rate our intelligence.

The movie habit, by which I mean going to the movies indiscriminately three or four times a week, must be injurious; it is bad for the human mind, which occasionally needs stimulation. To sit back passively and wait to be amused, and to do that as an occupation, can hardly be beneficial. Those who live the life of the mind, know that it is a more exciting life than any series of entertainments. And those who live the life of the mind enjoy *occasional* entertainments; as a vacation following work is more pleasant than a perpetual vacation.

There are three kinds of movies I especially enjoy: the two-hour film version of a great novel; exploration in wild or remote parts of the earth; elementary mirth. I am not ashamed of this—I love to see a seven-passenger car enter the plate-glass window of a drugstore; I love to see a pompous United States Senator hit in the face with a

custard pie; it does me good. I shall always be grateful
to Harold Lloyd, the funniest screen comedian I ever
saw.

But the screen versions of novels and dramas please
me more than anything else. I wonder who thought first
of putting "Little Women" on the screen. This story,
with Katharine Hepburn as Jo, is one of the greatest
successes in the history of the modern stage. After I had
seen it, I advised others to take with them, not a handker-
chief, but a tablecloth. What cataracts of tears! And yet
it is not a tragic or even a sad story; but there is something in its naturalness that melts the heart. As I came
out of the theatre, I met a sophisticated graduate of
Smith College, and in response to my question, she said,
"Oh, I sobbed from beginning to end." Our fourteen-year-
old boys and girls, who, one might have thought, would
have been bored or only mildly curious, were completely
bowled over. Not seven thousand as in ancient times, but
seventy million, made the response to the simple appeal.

It is good to learn at this moment that Katharine Hep-
burn is to appear in "The Little Minister" and that Hugh
Walpole is directing in America a screen version of
"David Copperfield." [1]

I learned to like full-length novels on the screen by
seeing, years ago, Victor Hugo's immortal "Les Misérables." [1] How I wish I might see it again. I probably
shall. With modern improvements it could be made even
more effective.

While evil pictures should be avoided, and their number will certainly be lessened by the strength of the public

[1] Since screened.

sentiment against them, it will not do to be too squeamish in the production of great novels, great dramas, or striking incidents in history.

In the dramatization of history, George Arliss excels; no one who saw it will ever forget his "Disraeli." Last summer I saw at Bad Axe, Michigan, his version of the Rothschilds. It is very fine. I would suggest as a first-class historical subject, the career of Lord Clive in India,[2] one of the most sensational series of events in the eighteenth century.

One of the greatest of the motion-picture producers— I wish I could remember which one—said some years ago: "The greatest writer for the movies who ever lived was Robert Browning." Browning invented more plots than any other writer, ancient or modern. In the early days of the movies, I saw a screen version of Browning's epic poem, "The Ring and the Book." That screen version was not well done; there is room now for a better one. Browning's play, "Pippa Passes," was put on the screen; and "A Blot in the 'Scutcheon" ought to be. If I were a movie producer, I would hire scenario-writers to prepare screen versions of the following poems by Browning: "A Forgiveness," "The Inn Album," "The Laboratory," "My Last Duchess," "A Light Woman," "The Pied Piper of Hamelin" (always room for another version of that story), "Porphyria's Lover," "Childe Roland to the Dark Tower Came," "Ivan Ivanovitch," and "Clive."

Stevenson's "Treasure Island," which appeared during the summer of 1934, was almost an ideal production; I

[2] Editor's note: Since the writing of this article, "The Little Minister," "David Copperfield" and "Clive of India" have been screened.)

have never witnessed any movie with more continual, sheer enjoyment than this. I was spellbound from beginning to end. I pay homage to the producers of this picture, because they spared no expense in the beauty and splendor of its production; and they gave absolutely an all-star cast. Every man, woman, and child ought to see this new version of "Treasure Island."

Among the great novels of all nations, besides the best of Dickens and Thackeray, I should like to see Sienkiewicz's "With Fire and Sword," "The Deluge," "Pan Michael," "The Knights of the Cross." Sienkiewicz was the famous Polish novelist who wrote "Quo Vadis"; and that of course was a popular production; but these other romances of his are just as well adapted to the screen.

It is high time for a new version of Cooper's "The Last of the Mohicans," and I would suggest these other novels by Cooper—"The Spy," "The Red Rover," "The Two Admirals," and "The Pilot," the last-named having as its hero John Paul Jones. Wilkie Collins's "Armadale" is just as exciting as "The Moonstone" and "The Woman in White," and these two novels by him have reached the screen.

Charles Reade's romantic masterpiece, "The Cloister and the Hearth," simply cries out for picture production. Kipling's short stories, especially "The Man Who Would Be King," are magnificent both for action and scenery.

Stevenson ought not to be represented only by "Treasure Island." I think that "The Black Arrow," "Kidnapped," "The Master of Ballantrae," "The Ebb Tide," and "The Beach of Falesa," would be marvelous pictures.

I do not know how many of Walter Scott's novels have

appeared on the screen but I think "Quentin Durward" would make a tremendous success. Thomas Hardy's "Far from the Madding Crowd" is perfectly adapted to the screen; and how about Thomas Hughes's "Tom Brown's School Days" doing for boys what "Little Women" did for girls?

Arnold Bennett's, "The Grand Babylon Hotel," has all the ingredients for a good picture—an American millionaire in London with his beautiful daughter, and plenty of adventure.

For sheer, continuous excitement, I have never read any novel that surpassed Louis Tracy's "The Wings of the Morning"; it would go well on the screen.

Among contemporary novels, I think "The Lamb in His Bosom" by Caroline Miller, "So Red the Rose" by Stark Young, and "Once a Wilderness" by Arthur Pound, ought to be filmed; they deal with scenes in American geography and history.

The tales of the Knights of the Round Table, as told by old Malory in "Morte d'Arthur" or by Tennyson, are full of potentialities for the screen; and has any one thought of "Gulliver's Travels," or "Pilgrim's Progress?"

In conclusion let me say it is better to praise good movies than to attack bad ones. It is better to see good movies than to see bad ones. It is better to see good movies than not to see any movies.

CHAPTER X

THE PARABLE OF THE CLIMBING GIRL

by

EDWIN SCHALLERT

To understand the phenomenon of censorship, as applied to the motion picture, one has to search into historic phases of this huge and elaborate art-industry. Few things are so closely related to the public mind as the film entertainment. Yet this same entertainment slowly, and almost surreptitiously insisted itself upon the world consciousness. Moving photography, as a medium for popular diversion, just grew, much after the manner of Topsy in "Uncle Tom's Cabin"; it was not plotted or designed for its great future, except possibly in the minds of its scientific advocates and inventors. Their vision, crystallized in that of Thomas Edison, foresaw from the beginning, even, the cinema with sound, but the men who sponsored the film's appeal to the populace were concerned with commercial objectives, and in most cases a quick and sure-fire traffic in a very alive and fascinating commodity.

An early and oft-quoted incident emphasizes the fact that the piquant attraction of the motion pictures seems perennially surpassing. Commodore J. Stuart Blackton, pioneer in the field, has often pointed to the fact that a rudimentary little advertisement, called "Girl Climbing a Tree," proved a source of triumphant revenue in the primitive peep-show days of what was later to become a great international enterprise. Noble achievements of even that early era like "U.S. Battleship at Sea" and "Joseph Jefferson in 'Rip's Sleep'" suffered in the monetary comparisons. It's "what the public wants" that rules the movies; but "what the public wants" is ever subject to changing analyses, though it seems to find its cadence often in that fundamental note—the crudely stated word, "Sex."

From those lesser sources of the peep-show days, with their crude intentions, and often equally crude audiences, many brooks, rivulets and even mighty rivers of progress have sprung. The motion picture's power today is expressed in terms ranging from thousands paid in individual weekly salaries to players and executives to millions invested in theatres, and in groups of pictures, and even occasionally the single picture. The empire today is world-wide; the intimate force of the output sometimes terrific, while Hollywood itself is a domain of glamour, a surprising influence, and strangely a magnate for the creator. All motion pictures that are circulated today are not made in Hollywood, but for all practical purposes this town on the sunlit Pacific Coast is the capital. It is the capital, at least (for good or ill), of most of the thought that goes into the filmic emprise, and also much of the inspiration. Isolated pictures emanating from other points are now and then successful, but they are the exceptions. The great pictures that have really made history are practically all of Hollywood origin.

Where one finds one "Private Life of Henry VIII" coming from England, one must view a veritable pageant from the days of "The Birth of a Nation" on, emanating from the sunshine-laden Cellulandia of Southern California.

To grasp the full significance of Hollywood itself, one must perhaps know the background of the place, and also what has happened there. However, for the purposes of this particular discussion, that would entail too lengthy a digression. This much can be said, though, that there is something of the locale itself that reaches the screen in the majority of its cinema productions. The more these are of the outdoors, perhaps, the more of Hollywood is in them. Something about the place seems to breed optimism. "It's the sunshine in the films that counts," a noted English author said to this writer recently; "that sunshine has caused the Hollywood picture to become popular all over the world. People derive an unconscious benefit from its influence. It's the reason the American output of screen entertainment is so universally esteemed by the general audience."

Really, there is nothing unhealthy in the fundamental atmosphere surrounding the so-called colony—which is neither a colony nor anything like it—of pictures. The actinic rays that fall on hillside and Coastal plain most days in the year are all for the good. They are life-giving in a physical way, and should be that mentally, as well. There is nothing effete or decadent, or even very much ultra, in the natural modes and manners of living in this light-bathed region, where the tone generally is subtropically quiescent.

Cities that are situated by the sea do not generally turn in on themselves; there is not that in-grafting of the moods of pleasure. Rather there is a reaching out. New York should feel the boon of the maritime expanse, and it does, though too much of the so-called culture in New York is confined to a narrow walled-in region in the general vicinity of Broadway and Forty-second Street. In Hollywood one looks out almost perpetually at green lawns and flower gardens. This is true even of certain of the modern studios, where nature is encouraged to furnish beauty and adornment. Such an atmosphere as this is, in many ways, well-nigh perfect. Given its chance the charm of such surroundings should bring rich fruit. And it does, much of the time, and under the best auspices. But then—just momentarily to turn whimsical —it might be remembered that a girl doesn't ascend a tree in a closed room, either, but in an apple or some other sort of orchard. The natural environment that can offer so much hygienic benefit, also has certain other delicately suggested possibilities.

This, of course, is all a purely imaginary implication of the Hollywood setting. There is romance in the air, at any rate, and a luxuriant influence that no doubt is felt in the creation of much screen drama. Pompiian and Helenic motifs are blended in movie studio *mise-en-scene*. They must, perhaps, often manifest themselves in certain forms of neo-paganism which appear to be relished by a neo-paganic world, and that need eventually a halt to be called, such as happened in the spring of a year ago.

The controversy between the Church and the Hollywood state is now dimming into a page of history, and it is not my purpose to go into it extensively in the course of this particular chapter. There have been earlier censorship wars, and there will be later ones, though the 1934 drive was in all respects the most serious up to the present time. What the whole world wonders in the long run is how much it has accomplished for film betterment— that is if the world at large does take a serious interest in that especial issue.

To begin with, moral turpitude is no singular and solitary possession of Hollywood itself. Whatever may be said of the place it doesn't make any speciality of vice, nor of virtue either. Neither does the rest of the world, except for certain cloistered communities, which devote themselves to the benefits of prayer and fasting, and certain also cloistered groups that do otherwise, the former for goodness, the latter for antipode.

Hollywood oftentimes almost seems to give itself over to a hopeless normalcy. Despite the rumors of wild parties, which have long been heard, its social life is in large part more quiet, more cultured, and certainly more interesting than the social life in many other spheres. It isn't the custom to become intoxicated in Hollywood otherwise than agreeably, if one becomes intoxicated at all. That isn't true of other worlds, even though the matter of drinking is somewhat more sanely pursued throughout America than prior to prohibition, or during portions of the period of supposed "National Abstinence." One hears reports of fistic encounters of an evening in movieland, implying bad behavior, but most of them when traced to their source are of trifling import. Temperamental people are bound occasionally to become somewhat excited.

Marital unsteadiness is apparently a black mark against Hollywood; but it is a black mark more in publicity than in fact. For every marriage that has failed there, nine or more have succeeded. Surely not a bad average, when the general census is taken. The divorce laws of California are not especially easy, though, of course, Mexico and Nevada are always near. But then today, with the airplane, they are near to every place in America.

The devil, wine and woman (why not man too?) are symbolically the chief causes of sin, and these have been disposed of as the primal reasons for any defection that may exist in Hollywood. At all events, it is trusted that wine and the woman have. The devil can never be dealt with completely.

There are then the world and the flesh to be considered, and of course that takes in the whole earthly panorama. "What do people want?" That is the question Hollywood most consistently asks. "What the public wants it gets," and thus we get back to our first thesis, "what the public wants rules the movies." Is the public for pictures in their graduate stage any different from the elementary that showed its preference for the lass that made the arboreal ascent in the peep-show days?

Probably one should proceed to answer this question by pointing immediately to Mae West. She climbed no trees, but she invited an ascent in order to see her. Whenever one is tempted to look down in what might be called a moral way on the screen, he is simultaneously lured to loftier level. That is one of the peculiar paradoxes.

Miss West's invitation, with its upward lift, may have been what set the films on their downward chute, censorially speaking, though no one exactly knows who fired the first shot at Sarajevo. It seems, however, to be the old paradox working. Miss West was nominated the queen of 1933, and right after that came the deluge as typified by the Legion of Decency. She was no more than the last straw, if she was that; the camel's back had already been bent to the point of breaking.

Censorship of pictures is a recurrent manifestation. It is part of the ebb and flow of their life. In 1908 or thereabouts the exhibitors of New York City all had their licenses taken away from them by the order of the Mayor. It was an early clean-up campaign. Because it was in part political—this censorship—the exhibitors fought it, and finally won. Simultaneously, and because of all the hubbub, the films themselves began to show some improvement. The easiest way is not always the best way to entice public favor. Sometimes the difficult way paves a better future. Censorship, a medicine, has frequently turned out to be a tonic.

When a series of disasters within the colony itself, that were of a rather scandalous nature, occurred in the early twenties, including the William Desmond Taylor murder, and the sudden death of Virginia Rappe, the pictures again took stock of themselves. Out of this time of trial and tribulation came "Robin Hood," "The Covered Wagon," "The Ten Commandments" and other highly representative and ambitious undertakings. These all helped to increase the more general prestige of pictures. They also were great box-office winners.

In 1935, following the Legion of Decency campaign, have emerged such productions as "David Copperfield," "Lives of a Bengal Lancer," "The Barretts of Wimpole Street," "The House of Rothschild," "Les Misérables" and other works of great merit. Stress seems to be exceedingly beneficial to pictures. Perhaps it focuses public attention on the screen; perhaps also—significant point— it awakens the public to its own best interests.

One wonders why the producers become slovenly about the character of their output of films. One may also wonder occasionally why the public seems to sink to slovenliness in its own taste. There are probably much the same unsubstantial causes for both conditions. The world changes; it slumps, and it picks up again. Shakespeare the poet-dramatist was followed by the crude and carnal Restoration period. Incipient Shakespeares of the movies are often succeeded apparently by a crew of lusty and roistering scribes and Pharisees who offer gilt for gold. And the public, in its acceptance, veers curiously between them.

Fortunately there are quicker means of checking up motion pictures than ever prevailed in any other form of expression. The stage has gone to the dogs with salaciousness of a sort; it will probably take a considerable time for it to recover. Literature also has become super-realistic, to put it mildly. There are few places where the torch burns today, and if there is any place where it does burn at all it is in some of the better pictures produced in Hollywood since the coming of the new dawn—and in the more abstract realm, let us say, of music.

Pictures can serve a high and ennobling purpose with a "Copperfield," a "Lives of the Bengal Lancer" and a "Les Misérables" and they can also reap a large revenue. Would these have been popular films when audiences were in the mood for Mae West pre-eminently? It is hard to say. The answer is "the world changes."

There is a high ideal that Hollywood could express if it should ever come to it, and that is to set the standards of taste relentlessly, fearlessly, and without regard to the demands of the counting house; but then the films do not happen to be either a subsidized art or a super-capitalized industry. Furthermore, black must sometimes be contrasted with the white. All pictures cannot be moulded in one crucible. The public has a way of becoming wearied with even too much decency.

More solid and sounder values necessarily are accumulated out of a period of depression and pictures lagged a little behind in following a national change. Audiences awakened considerably in advance of the studios themselves. They had ceased going to the theatre with their wonted regularity. The public was re-estimating its life in new terms, and will probably continue to do so of necessity. Other changes in taste, and methods of satisfying that taste are destined to follow. Even the Legion of Decency rules on acceptances will not remain quite the same; it may be anticipated that the vigilance will gradually be relaxed.

Slowness of pictures in responding to the altered public mood during the depression was in part due to extraordinary prevailing conditions. The talking film, it must be remembered began to assume its full sway only about the spring of 1929, which year later witnessed the stock market collapse.

Pictures "rode along" on the stimulus of the sound innovation for much longer than did other industries following the market collapse. With the coming of sound they also absorbed a host of new influences, and the bulk of these were what is known as sophisticated influences. Probably ninety per cent of the new people who came into the studios were from New York's Broadway, and they brought with them the modern ultra-realistic stage tradition, which viewed profanity as no crime in the theatre, and daringly and frequently suggestive themes as entirely feasible of exploitation.

These "new ideas" came to some extent to be promulgated in pictures, but these pictures were not being presented to simply a select coterie in a twelve-hundred seat theatre; they were being given to Oshkosh, Cedar Rapids, Baton Rouge and all way places. What the out-of-town half-holidaying buyers welcomed with glee on the Gay White Way, the green-pasturing and Main-Streeting folk viewed with uncertainty and then alarm. The movie theatre was certainly getting to be a place where one "could not take the children." It isn't yet in each instance, but then there is more of an attempt to classify pictures.

Not all the people who objected to pictures lived in small towns. A number of them were of that large conservative and respectable group who dwell in all large cities. These, too, found the nature of Hollywood's output more or less distasteful. It was especially difficult to find any place where the offspring might be parked on a Saturday afternoon. I know I met one of my own contemporaries with his brood once on that day who said he'd been to a dozen theatres trying to locate one with a fitting show for his youngsters.

The temptation to use peppery, and occasionally even half-vulgar dialogue, had become very great. Pictures being more down-to-earth in a fundamental way as entertainment, couldn't be dressed up in a literary sense quite as much as the stage play. They had to favor the more elemental values. And they went to the extreme of mistaking *crude* for elemental. The net result was more errors in taste than anything else. Such bad taste, and a degree of pandering, were reflected also in the screen advertising.

That particular screen age is perhaps now fully ended. And the period that immediately followed, when the stop sign was raised, rank a momentary risk of inanity. But that too is passing. The immediate losses occasioned to pictures because of the Legion of Decency drive can scarcely be estimated in terms of dollars, but it is supposed that they are somewhere around ten million dollars. Few films were actually shelved, though one or two did meet that fate, including "Frankie and Johnny" produced in New York, which has recently been revised; but many productions were put on the banned roster which were completed before the Hays office could set its machinery of self-censorship entirely in motion.

The war carried on by the Legion of Decency was for a time quite relentless, and Class "C" lists contained a fairly high proportion of the *verboten* features. Actually there haven't been more than half-a-dozen films since the better operation of the code of morals, administered by the Hays organization, that have gotten into trouble. The Catholic Church has objected to one or two of these on grounds peculiar to its own religious organization, and the code administration of the industry is not attempting to censor films simply from the Catholic standpoint.

The fact that Joseph I. Breen, in charge of the code administration, was able to take a vacation in Europe in the late spring and early summer of 1935, was perhaps indication that progress was being made in handling a much vexed situation. In the beginning Breen did nearly all the work alone, while later on a "brain trust" composed of theatrical men, newspaper men and welfare workers was formed.

Breen himself is known as a strict dictator, one who could enforce rules by determination and personality, as well as authority, and his ideas of story reconstruction, when particularly difficult problems were encountered, must have proved rather good, because one or two concerns made him proffers as producer of pictures.

Undoubtedly the Hays office does everything possible, from watching the initial script to supervising the final cutting, to prevent a film from being banned either by itself or the Legion of Decency, and undoubtedly, too, most of the producers tried rather desperately to toe the mark of self-autonomy, but it is understood that the victories had not always been accomplished without conflict. It's give and take in the long run, and concessions from a too-strict order are probably also being made by the censoring forces.

To some extent, the zest in producing was impeded in

Hollywood, a circumstance which was added to by the threats of severe tax legislation. But all in all, the Legion of Decency drive has been a prod and a spur to the industry, whose fullest benefits, while already somewhat understood, will not be entirely realized, nor completely forgotten, for some time to come.

There is always the danger that pictures might slip back into their old cycle, but it is lessening, and in general the films are likely in the next few years—and barring some sudden revolutionary effect resembling television—to show their greatest progress.

All will not and cannot be right in Hollywood until the output of films is curtailed, or until the machinery of the studios at large is geared up to produce a larger quantity of first class motion pictures. It may be doubted whether the amount of fine material completely to fill the huge movie maw year after year exists, when the full complement of productions is reckoned at approximately five hundred films annually.

There is more of a tendency, of course, today, to bring films into America from other lands—Great Britain being the primary source, because it can supply them in English. If the British output can be increased that may augment the improvement. Still, so far, England more than America (Hollywood), has had vast trouble of making pictures of international interest. Hollywood has great advantages in the study it has given to the world market, the cosmopolitan nature of its personnel, and the efficiency of its system of production.

Hollywood has great absorbtive powers. Naught that is in the least adaptable to the films but is used in some way at some time. Even setbacks, be they censorial or otherwise, are generally transmuted into advantages in the ultimate outcome. The resiliency of the studio center is, in most respects, remarkable and has been surprisingly demonstrated during the time the films were placed on trial.

CHAPTER XI

THE BANKRUPTCY OF CINEMA AS ART

by

SEYMOUR STERN

"The movie producers, being men of low intelligence and even lower courage, refused to experiment."—Gilbert Seldes, *The Movies and the Talkies.*

"The American film industry has above all lacked originality, courage and resource. It has left such things to the despised Scandinavians, Germans, and Russians."—John Gould Fletcher, *The Crisis of the Film.*

"When the Future of Hell is written in this series, a large number of pages will have to be reserved for the Americans who make films."—Ernest Betts, *Heraclitus, or the Future of Films.*

Twenty years after *The Birth of a Nation,* nineteen years after *Intolerance,* and ten after *Potemkin,* the cinema as a fine art, in every country of the world, presents a picture of absolute bankruptcy. In those countries, notably Germany and the Soviet Union, where within the last decade the most promising and fruitful creative developments were witnessed, today there exists absolutely nothing which can be considered as evidence of a noble use of the film as an instrument of creative expression. The initial promise of the German cinema, projected during the early '20s in a number of films of a high order of excellence—*The Last Laugh, Variety, Siegfried, Kriemhild's Revenge, Dr. Mabuse, The Golem, Secrets of the Soul, The Street, Vanina,* Lubitsch's *The Loves of Pharoah* and *Sumurun, Caligari,* Buchowetzki's *Danton,* etc.—was forced to remain unfulfilled: the German cinema, the first important one to develop on the European continent, had already fallen into a condition of premature decay at least five years before Hitler came into power. By 1933 little was left of it to be destroyed by the Nazis, and it is said that their use of the film for purposes of war propaganda has proved singularly dull, ineffective and beneath the standards of the lowest American commercialism.

In the U. S. S. R.—the only country that can boast a film university—the picture is almost as dismal. In 1925 Eisenstein's *Potemkin* marked the beginning of the golden age of the Soviet cinema. This epochal film was to Soviet film art what Griffith's *The Birth of a Nation* was to the cinema in general: the first major creative achievement. In the subsequent five years there emerged in the Workers' and Peasants' Republic at least three directors of extraordinary creative ability—Sergei Eisenstein, Vsevolod Pudovkin and Alexander Dovzhenko—and there appeared, both by them and by their students and followers, at least a dozen other films—*Ten Days That Shook the World, Old and New, The End of St. Petersburg, Mother, Storm Over Asia, Arsenal, Earth, A Fragment of an Empire, The New Babylon, Old Siberia, China Express, Turk-Sib,* and others—which collectively represent the greatest advance in the field of cinematic art since the masterpieces of David Wark Griffith. Sometime around 1930, this torrential Russian outburst of creativity began to slacken.

Today, a mere decade after the production of *Potemkin,* it is a matter of common observation that Eisenstein, Pudovkin and Dovzhenko, though alive and in excellent health, have practically stopped producing films in the land of the Soviets. Not a single other Russian director has arisen who even remotely approaches any one of these three in originality and power, and the best that contemporary Soviet production can offer may be seen in such meagre tripe as *The Youth of Maxim* and in such meretricious or hopelessly ordinary films as *Three Songs About Lenin, Petersburg Nights* and the much-vaunted *Chapayev.* Whatever the reasons, the fact remains that film art in any large and ample sense of the term, is now a thing of the past, perhaps also of the future, in the Soviet Republic. But it is *not* a thing of the present there.

Casting a swift eye across the rest of Europe, we see nothing in the form of significant creative filmwork that deserves even passing notice. The commercial cinemas of England and the Continent continue to grind out their heavy-handed imitations of the standardized Hollywood program product. Up to a few years ago, this dreary spectacle was relieved on occasion by isolated French productions (not to mention the German art-cinema at the height of its glory) of a definite creative calibre— *Finis Terrae, The Fall of the House of Usher, David Golder, The Little Match Girl, Faces of Children, Tragedy of the Street, Poil de Carotte,* etc.—and by the enthusiastic constructive activity of the English film societies and film magazines. But today, no alternatives to the market-junk of the big commercial European film companies gladden the eye. The French experimental cinema has been dead for at least three years; no single picture equal in esthetic merit or in sincerity of conception to *The Passion of Joan of Arc,* or to the earlier *Crainquebille,* has been put forth in France or elsewhere on the Continent; no spectacle of a dignity and significance remotely comparable to that of the early *Monna Vanna,* the greatest of all European mass-films, has even been attempted within the past five years; Rene Clair, who at best is absurdly overrated, has long degenerated into a formula; and the film-art movement of England, which barely managed to summon up enough energy two years ago to register a feeble and belated protest against Upton Sinclair's destruction of Eisenstein's Mexican film,[2] today is all but a pleasant memory of yesteryear. In a word, while the European film industries continue uninterruptedly with their programs of popular drivel and their desperate duplications of Hollywood, the European cinema as a creative force in Western civilization is utterly and hopelessly dead.

If we turn to the United States, we may possibly expect to find a very different state of affairs here: America, after all, is the birthplace of the motion picture: it was America

[2] For the benefit of readers not familiar with the details of Eisenstein's Mexican film: The film-epic of Mexico originally known as *"Que Viva Mexico!"* was privately financed by Mr. and Mrs. Upton Sinclair and a few of their friends during the Russian director's sojourn in America in 1931–32. After the production was completed, Sinclair had the entire negative of 232,000 feet edited, under his own supervision, by an independent commercial producer. Eisenstein's original intention was ignored, the original conception of *"Que Viva Mexico!"* hopelessly distorted, and the negative indiscriminately mutilated. Sinclair's handiwork was released as *Thunder Over Mexico.* The outrage was vigorously protested by radicals, intellectuals and art-lovers everywhere; in Mexico, Sinclair's market-version was banned after threat of a general strike by Mexican labor. The original negative, however, has not yet been saved. This catastrophe definitely marks the end of a long period of splendidly creative filmwork throughout the world.

that produced Griffith, the first creative force in this medium. But we are slated to receive a great disappointment if we entertain any notions that the American cinema, creatively considered, is in a better condition than the current European or Soviet cinema. Griffith has ceased to be the "dominant mind" (as Gilbert Seldes once called him), *i.e.,* the single major creative influence, of the American screen, after twenty years of unchallenged ascendancy; Stroheim, for all his titanic labors on *Greed,* today struggles for dictatorship; and the original crowd of cloak-and-suit manufacturers who gained possession of the industry in its pioneer days—before it had half a chance to realize a fraction of the creative aims and functions envisioned for it by its early enthusiasts—are more solidly in the saddle of power than ever before.—It is worse today because now they have the big bankers behind them, who lend financial and strategic support to their position. Their regimentation of Hollywood, of those working on their payrolls, has been complete: they have successfully suppressed any single creative mind that might get out of hand and attempt to use the cinema according to some other, possibly more civilized, conception than their own. It is *their* tradition of filmmaking, *their* interpretation of what the public wants, *their* tastes and standards that have triumphed. Except for a handful of intelligent but futile sub-producers, they have peopled their studios, from executive office to "prop" department, with their own kind.

As the special concern of this essay is with the American rather than with the world cinema, it will be worthwhile to examine more closely the present condition of the medium in this country and to make a sweeping survey of the causes which have led to its debasement.

Even a superficial inspection of contemporary American cinema reveals certain inescapable features. First of all, no conceivable mental gymnastics can lead one to imagine that a film *art* worthy of the name exists here today. Every consistent student of the motion picture knows that the present period of American cinema represents a distinct degeneration from the period dominated by Griffith. Between *The Birth of a Nation* (1915) and *Isn't Life Wonderful?* (Griffith's last important picture, released in 1925), there appeared a number of works of major value—*Intolerance, Broken Blossoms, America,* Stroheim's *Greed,*—to which there are not even near-counterparts today. These remain unrivalled save by the grand masterpieces of the silent Soviet cinema: possibly also, with reservations, by a few isolated independent productions such as Murnau's *Tabu.* Already five years before the advent of the talk-film, a rank misconception of the nature of film-montage [3] had gained ascendancy over the formal creative experimentations of Griffith, and when *Isn't Life Wonderful?* appeared—I consider it the last serious creative film-work to have been done in the United States—it failed at the box-office: though it contained superficially popular elements, its subtly formalized treat-

[3] Montage: For the benefit of readers to whom this term is new, it will suffice to define it here as the formative creation, through the agency of film-cutting, of the movements and rhythms of the photographed film and their organization into a continuity-pattern. The creative act, or process, of film-montage is the very essence of cinematic art. In Hollywood the term has been characteristically distorted to mean something to which it has absolutely no relation: *i.e.,* a short transitional or connective sequence consisting of a rapid jumble of trick shots photographed from unusual angles.

ment of the material could not compete with the smooth, brilliant, and highly polished surface-finish of such un-cinematic bits of persiflage as Lubitsch's sex comedies (how inferior, by the way, to his fine filmwork in Germany), or with such pseudo-artistic concoctions as Murnau's *Sunrise* and King Vidor's *The Crowd*.

After 1925 Griffith's decline was rapid and complete. His elemental, but exciting and dramatically adequate, formal methods were superseded, first by the dubious camera-tricks which marred even the best of the German films and which inevitably captured the fancy of the Hollywood people, who used the new "foreign" devices to spice up their stereotypes product; and a short time later, by the great Russian silent films, where his methods of photography and cutting were realized to the *n*th degree and developed, at least in some instances, into entirely new forms. Since Griffith's decline as the foremost American director, it is a simple matter to trace the progressive artistic degradation of the American film. Unfortunately, space does not permit of such details as would make a review of this process dramatically exciting to the film student. Six months ago Seldes informed the readers of Scribner's magazine that in the past five years, *i.e.*, since the inception of the talk-film, not a single picture of the highest order of importance had been produced in the United States. If to this statement be added the fact that Griffith's style-form (the first in the history of the cinema) has not been supplanted here by any other equally potent formal development, but has merely been followed by a strictly utilitarian, cut-and-dried technique, of doubtful esthetic value, and which for the most part does not belong to the medium, the creative bankruptcy of the latter can be duly estimated.

However, this condition is neither freakish nor ephemeral, as may be the case at present in Russia, nor is it a mere temporary setback to a normally abundant artistic growth. Its roots, I believe, are fixed fast in the sub-soil of the American screen world—in the calibre of personality that prevails among the film-makers themselves, and ultimately, of course, in the mentality of American audiences. Simply stated, the fundamental cause amounts to the failure of the American film people to apprehend the real powers, capacities and resources of the cinema, beyond those necessary to a standardized, straightforward narrative technique. Their failure may be partially explained in that the majority of them, particularly the directors, cameramen and executives, are not, and have never been, essentially of the cinema. Essentially they are vaudevillians, stage people, circus people, manufacturing people, shrewd merchants, but not, except in a small number of instances, people who were "born to the element." It is certainly significant that they refer to themselves as "showmen," and to the cinema as the "show business." For while they have managed the mechanical apparatus with professional skill, the technical and artistic culture of the film, its revolutionary traditions, its untouched creative capacities, its inherent potentialities as a thing freed from theatre, from painting, and from literature,—these have all escaped them, the very issues implicit in these phases of cinema remaining as foreign to their experience as a book of Chinese verse. Thus, it is no wonder that every new Russian or German or French film of creative significance takes them by surprise, sweeps them off their feet, dazzles, frightens them: they had never suspected these new forms, these fresh, yet easily conceivable ways of picturizing content, these new patterns of photographic style and filmic continuity. A *Potemkin*, a *Ten Days That Shook the World*, a *Passion of Joan of Arc*, a *Cabinet of Dr. Caligari*, Tisse's photographic work on "*Que Viva Mexico!*"—such products of creative ingenuity and experimental daring shock and bewilder the Hollywood practitioners who, with, or perhaps despite, their wealth of resources and studio-machinery, have not managed to conceive a single new form of montage-relationships in all the years that have passed since *Intolerance*. The industry's one experiment along these lines was the Fox film, *The Power and the Glory* (1933). In spite of the solemnity of certain critics who praised it, this picture was a sadly half-baked attempt to dramatize the retrospect of a man's life by projecting its salient episodes in *non*-chronological order,—a departure from the simple, straight-line structure of traditional American continuity, which amounted to nothing more than Fejos' *The Last Moment* in a new framework, with two or three sequences placed "out of order" (as the Fox people explained it) to lend "novelty" to the retrospect. In itself this device was merely one of half a dozen radical measures of the same category which Griffith invented as far back as 1916 when he designed *Intolerance* on four parallel lines of sectional flash-backs and united the separate climaxes in a single gigantic filmic rhythm. The industry's film, made by professional experts, failed:

the juggling around of the retrospect episodes was not dramatically sagacious or psychologically imperative; on the screen it merely demonstrated what had been in the minds of its creators from the first,—a pointless, and somewhat vulgar, novelty. But *Intolerance,* a work achieved independently of the American film industry, was no mere showman's novelty. Conceived and executed as a creative experiment, it projected a system of image-relationships—rhythm and counterpoint, present action and retrospect, detail and totality, close up and perspective—in a grand architectonic design which became, under Griffith's direction, a cinematic fugue. Yet this monumental work, the supreme masterpiece of the American screen, dates back practically twenty years— when the movies were "in their infancy":—how can it be maintained, as it is today by a few misguided critics and intellectuals, that the American film has advanced as an art-form when in the interim it has not dared one-tenth as much as this? The point is, of course, that it has not only not advanced: it has definitely retrogressed. For in the beginning there was Griffith; but today what is there? —Standardized routine continuity; standardized photography; standardized laboratory process; mock realism; artificial landscapes; a submergence per formula of all pictorial elements inherent in any given story; and, as a crowning feature of Hollywood professionalism, the trick transitional or connective sequence, with standardized "montage" by Vorkapich—a sample of the "influence" of Soviet film technique on American film production!

It is an unalterable principle of esthetic criticism that no art actually progresses except as it learns to express itself in its own native terms. On this basis, the American screen, creatively viewed, is hardly entitled to the grandiose claims of "progress" which its publicity departments and its deluded magnates are continually making for it. "No new form of art," writes Fletcher, "has ever been brought into the world under such favorable circumstances as has the film; and no new form of art has so little justified its claim to be ranked as an art at all. That is the extraordinary paradox that lies at the root of all discussion of cinema art." At any rate, no art has ever been so heavily financed; but to what advantage even at its experimental best?—*David Copperfield?* This embarrassingly overrated film was neither fish nor fowl: (1) it was only midling Dickens, and (2) it was decidedly poor cinema. The hopeless state of film criticism in this country is beautifully demonstrated by the acclaim with which this picture was received in the more unsophisticated intellectual circles. *Crime without Passion?* Can this piece—so far superior to the Hollywood product, yet so far beneath even the minor achievements of world-cinema—possibly be admitted as a "contribution?"[4] *Our Daily Bread?* Was it not a shame to waste this excellent title? . . . In brief, the best "bold," "audacious," "different," "experimental" attempts that Hollywood dares to offer are easily put to shame by a Soviet documentary film, a German legend-picture, a French *surrealiste* work. It

---

[4] *The Informer?* Much was heard through the industry in praise of this film: the experts had forgotten, or probably had never known, Grüne's *The Street*, the San Francisco sequences of *Greed*. Though unquestionably the most distinguished American picture of the current year, it was nevertheless not in any degree the masterpiece that critics, "experts" and newcomers to the screen imagined it, and after several viewings one wondered whether the director's accidental moment of filmic consciousness could be repeated.

cannot be otherwise. For to their ignorance on a multitude of intellectual and artistic matters, the Hollywood film people add ignorance of the powers and capacities of their own medium; to a superficial knowledge of elementary film technique, even the best of them fail to apply a willingness to experiment. A few camera tricks, some very good photography and lighting in their own native style, a vague notion that montage means "trick transitions" or "a lot of quick cuts,"—this is the full extent both of the knowledge and of the practice, by Hollywood, of cinema as art.

All this leads to the conclusion that in at least one respect the Hollywood people have scored a major victory. One traditional intention, heroically sustained since the earliest days of the film industry, has been realized at last—with a literalness and a consistency that are positively breath-taking. This is the age-old dream of the Hollywood movie crowd, executives and directors alike, to make the screen the living duplicate of the stage. Stupendous triumph! No longer need they wrestle with the stringent dynamic exigencies of the silent, black-and-white film! Today the talk-film, color-film, depth-film make feasible a literal, a devastatingly absolute transplantation of the stage onto the screen, and—think of it!—Broadway can be brought to Middletown! . . . This was the dream, the one serious longing of the movie magnates (apart from money), that animated all their efforts in the earliest days, that later caused them to hire renowned stage directors in the face of Griffith's repeated demonstrations of the future of the motion picture along native lines of development. But Griffith's films, which should have taught them everything, taught them nothing beyond elementary lessons in the technique of climax-construction—the best things in his films were too subtle and delicate; they were not adaptable to story-treatment of a cheaper fibre. True, the movie people stood in awe of *The Birth of a Nation*—(they have maintained a decent respect for it down the years principally because of the eighteen million dollars' profit which it brought in)· —but from Griffith's other important pictures, especially those (*Intolerance* and *Broken Blossoms*) from which they should have taken a cue as to the further development of film technique, they learned exactly nothing. Even the more obvious mechanical innovations which came in abundance from Griffith in the earlier days, were slow in penetrating. Thus, they saw *Intolerance,* with its myriad moving-camera shots, yet they did not see it: five years later, when the German films took them by storm, they became aware of the moving-camera, which they promptly hailed as a German invention![5] This slowness in utilizing new cinematic devices has not been a characteristic of American film activity during the past five years. A multitude of effective innovations are in use today.—But

[5] Readers not familiar with the history of the American film industry may find it difficult to appreciate this delicious bit of irony. The joke consists in Griffith's introduction of advanced styles of moving-camera shots in the Babylonian and modern episodes of *Intolerance,* produced in 1916. Hollywood, with the wealth of a kingdom behind it, ignored this new device by the leading American director, and waited for five years until the Germans, with practically no production-money to speak of, copied the device *ad nauseum* and sent it back under the banner of German studio craftsmanship! The American producers thereupon reproached their directors for not having thought of it first themselves! This is only one of a thousand examples of that phenomenal opaqueness which has characterized the· "picture-minds" of the professional Hollywood experts from the first days of the industry to the present.

their use is appallingly superficial; they are surface-ornaments of the film. No revolutionary organic change has come into the humdrum technique of film production in America.

Of course, underlying this barbarous indifference to the evolution of the motion picture along its only legitimate path has always been Hollywood's notorious obsession with the idea of turning the screen into a living replica of the stage. Already in 1921, only five years after the release of *Intolerance,* the Hollywood crowd was consciously striving to break away from any and all forms of film-montage that tended to shorten the individual shot and extend the dynamics of the shot into complex forms of shot-relationship. Griffith's use of overtone in *Broken Blossoms* (anticipating Eisenstein and Pudovkin by nearly ten years) meant as little to them as if it had never existed. This was not the sort of evolution the movie magnates had in mind when they screamed to the public about the "progress" of the industry. The kind of progress they meant was precisely the progressive approximation of film technique to the technique of the speaking stage. Thus, though Griffith had created thousands of separate shots in *The Birth of a Nation* and *Intolerance*—(despite the immense number of subtitles, both these pictures are impeccable models of continuity-pattern and filmic rhythm)—the movie crowd of the '20s, as if animated by a perverse instinct, argued that this basis of film-construction was wrong. Why mount the separate elements of a movement in a series of related images when you can show the movement in its entirety in one or two general shots? Rhythm?—Rhythm? That's really Art, isn't it? Then why bother with it? . . . Their reasoning, such as it was, ran very much along this line. The result was—the lengthening of the individual shot on the screen *nearly a decade before the actual invention of the talk-film.* Almost any American production during the period of the 1920's, if examined today, will testify to this progressive degeneration in continuity-form (since the time of Griffith's major filmwork), with its corresponding loss in dramatic vitality. The Hollywood people went blithely ahead, holding the shot on the screen immeasurably longer than Griffith's incorruptible cinematic instinct had ever allowed him to hold it even in his bad pictures, and through this practice, utterly devastating in its effect on the formal principles established by Griffith, other idiocies set in: The most glaring of these was the reduction to a minimum of the number of *detail shots.*—Attention to significant detail, which is a characteristic of all true creative expression, is to this day consistently avoided in Hollywood pictures. Second: the elimination of practically all *close ups* except those featuring the "star."—It ought to be plain to everyone that a voluptuous concentration on the superficial glamour of the featured players of a film is hardly provocative of an intelligent response.—Third: an extensive, and frequently wholesale, substitution of the *lap-dissolve* for the direct cut in almost every American film from 1925 down to the present.—No technical knowledge is required to realize that when an endless number of shots "melt" (dissolve) into each other in slow "mixes," without regard to the tempo of the action in each shot, the rhythm of the continuity is bound to suffer. But rhythm, which is the moving spirit of Art, is a minus quantity in Hollywood. Its existence has hardly been suspected by the experts. Fourth: increased use of the *trick shot* for its own sake to compensate (at intervals) for the slowing down of the cutting-pace of the picture.—In contrast, note the work of two stylists, Griffith and Stroheim. Note the extremely sparing, and then very cunning, use of any kind of trick shot in Griffith's films; the practically complete absence of trick shots in *Greed*. Montage, which merely means the system of relationship between the shots, is practically cancelled out of existence when the continuity is dominated by trick shots.—In short, what happened may be summed up as—a general *alteration* of the technique of picture-making to meet the requirements of the "make-the-screen-like-the-stage" idea, which demanded smoothness in place of dynamics, surface-finish in place of significant emphasis, clever transitional "effects" in place of organic structural development of the whole continuity.

By 1930, the mechanical realization of the talk-film invention relieved the Hollywood people of the burdensome necessity of creating *silent* talk-films through subtitles and sustained shots, as they had been doing for years during the "silent era." Arrival of the apparatus—they had been waiting for it eagerly since the beginning—was merely a signal to adjust themselves from what had been talk-films in effect to films that talked in actuality: the "revolution," as the publicity departments termed it, was a quite bloodless and easy affair—because in reality it was no revolution at all! In one of the early talkies, *The Letter,* single shots of characters speaking run on the screen for four and five minutes at a time. This was a great step "ahead";—in the silent days it would have been necessary to intercut these same shots with at least two or three subtitles, and none of the shots would have lasted on the screen for more than about one minute (a long time as screen-action goes). Now, thanks to *actual* speech, it was possible to reduce both camera and cutting to their minimum functions—the nearest step yet made toward their complete eradication. Today, five years after the appearance of the invention, the length of the average shot in the average Hollywood picture has been slightly shortened again—cutting is slightly more frequent. But by no stretch of the imagination can it be held that, in making a picture under Hollywood studio restrictions (other limitations aside), it is either feasible or permissible for a director to mount a film with emphasis on the cutting-pace or with subordination of dialogue to continuity-pattern and filmic rhythm. On the eve of the final victory (*i.e.,* perfection of the three-dimensional film) of the "make-the-screen-like-the-stage" idea, these lines by Gilbert Seldes, written many years ago, have a resounding pertinence:

"It ought to have been clear to everyone that the alliance between the stage and the screen was a mistake. It had actually failed. But its effect persisted. This muddle-headed idea that because the screen *could* use the material and the people of the stage, it was at its best when doing so, is responsible for the retarded development of the movie in America, giving it, at the age of twenty-five, the mentality of a child of six. . . . Like a child brought up in a dark room, it shrank from the light, like a cripple it preferred not to move. And light and movement are its life." (*The Movies and the Talkies,* p. 54.)

The Hollywood people have never been impressed by such strictures. They cannot conceive of taking Film seriously, that is, as Art, and there is something faintly ironical in the fact that the volumes of analytical material which have been written on the motion picture during the past twenty years have completely escaped them. To-day, with the three-dimensional film practically ready for use, they await its arrival with something akin to the excitement of a child who expects a new toy:

"It will mean that we will not need so many close-ups in our movies as we use today (*sic*). Now we must bring the camera close to the face of the actor to show the important emotions. But with the actors standing out clearly and roundly, as in our three-dimensional experiments, we can keep our camera back and follow them, *like on a stage,* and each motion will be clearly recorded." (N. Y. *Times,* January 20, 1935. Italics mine.)

This statement by Gregg Toland, one of the leading cameramen of Hollywood, may be taken as representative of the attitude of the entire industry. The statement would be complete had he added that their enthusiasm for the three-dimensional film has nothing whatever to do with the possibilities of its amplifying the resources of film-montage, but is due solely to the realization that this invention will literally fulfill the American producers' dream of making the screen resemble the stage to the *n*th degree of similitude. . . .

After the foregoing rather wholesale condemnation of the American cinema, it would seem only fair and an evidence of plain common sense to add a word of appraisal of the Hollywood entertainment-film as such,— *i.e.,* not as serious art; in other words, to give the devil his due. If it is true that Hollywood as an institution is the enemy of real art, of Culture *per se,* it is also true that, purely as a popular entertainment catering to an inevitably shallow vein of sentiment, the Hollywood product during the past five or six years has undergone a great improvement. (Incidentally, this improvement has come about wholly within the industry itself and in spite of the repressive influence of those perennial pests, the Church and the censor boards, which continue to have a deplorable effect on film-making in this country.) Taken for what it is, the American entertainment-film stands today as the best of its kind in the world. Compare the average Hollywood picture with the average European program product: the superiority of the former is overwhelming and beyond dispute. Of course, this may be merely another way of saying that one brand of poison is better than other brands of the same poison; but, however you choose to look at it, the fact remains that the Hollywood movie is immeasurably superior to its many imitations throughout the world. True, the pretentious vacuities of Josef "von" Sternberg and the lumbering theatrics of Cecil B. De Mille are still here; but over and against these, the more modern type of picture represents a new set of values that is greatly in advance of the formulae of the older showmen.

The brilliant advances in surface-finish and in swiftness, economy, and ingenuity of plot that have been made since the advent of the talkie are a matter of striking observation. These are the qualities thanks to which the American entertainment-film justly outshines its rivals on the world market. It possesses most of the good points of any fine manufactured product, such as a car, a refrigerator or an aluminum utensil. It is efficiently contrived and put together; it fits its purpose as a popular emotional excitant, just as these articles fulfill a universal utility, and, like these, it possesses immense, if superficial, physical attractiveness.[6] A beautiful example of a common program-picture that hits the high watermark of this type of mechanical excellence was *The Mystery Woman,* produced by Fox Films early in 1935. The story of this film was the usual slick affair devised out of a most plausible improbability and lubricated throughout by a perfectly ubiquitous cleverness. Hundreds of such products are turned out of the Hollywood factories. At best these pictures manifest a vigilant attention to dramatic efficacy, which, however, more often than not degenerates into the mere opportunism of melodrama but which at least has the minimum virtue of keeping audiences awake. Like all popular art, much vitality, much spontaneous dash and animation, together with much that is meretricious and hackneyed, goes into the content of these films; like all popular art, they belong to "the people." As such they are naturally full of a primitive optimism: not infrequently, as in films of the type of *Seventh Heaven* and *Life Begins,* they seem almost grotesque in their amiable acceptance of the bitterest tragedies. Such at-

[6] The strictly utilitarian function of the Hollywood "entertainment" film cannot be sufficiently emphasized. Consider, for example, the increasing output of propaganda pictures for war and fascism. These pictures, glorifying the army, the navy, the gangster-police, the right of the individual to acquire wealth through the exploitation of others, etc., may be so much rubbish, culturally speaking, but they are supremely effective in sustaining the prestige of the ruling class at times when the American system speeds to ruin. Like the Church, Hollywood serves its prescribed utilitarian mission—in the interests of wealth, war and the psychological enslavement of the populace.

titudes, however, are quite in keeping with the dominant quality of the Hollywood product—surface-finish: *i.e.,* the sensuous lushness with which each scene is pictorially realized. The seductive glamour of physical objects in these films—clothes, furniture, automobiles, drawing-rooms, not to mention the complexion and figures of the screen stars—is considered the supreme triumph of Hollywood photographers and laboratories. Like refrigerators, automobiles and kitchen utensils, their product must "sell."

In this regard arises the question of whether or not the superficial progress of the Hollywood film warrants a shift in critical attitude. It is the fashion nowadays, especially among the young intellectuals who write for the liberal magazines, to temporize agreeably with current film production, and they have even managed to discover a number of self-styled "classics" in the course of their new rapport with the industry. Thus, we find them acclaiming a picture like *It Happened One Night* as a "classic of the American screen." *It Happened One Night* was, in effect, a delightfully spontaneous and charming picture, not without its priceless moments of humor. However, it is absolutely certain that it will not be remembered five years hence; as comedy, neither the film nor the mind behind it transcended the framework of strictly popular values. This fact alone, as every developed critic knows, is sufficient to damn any effort that becomes a candidate for the title of a work of art. But the acclaim which this and similar pictures receive from the intellectuals is painful evidence of the laxness and vague-mindedness of American film criticism. Even the most picture-wise of the New York newspaper critics, (usually excepting Andre Sennwald) who ordinarily may be expected to know better, take a cue from the bright boys of the liberal press: it is not uncommon to find them writing solemnly about the "style" of such directors as Milestone, Sternberg, Capra, Boleslavsky, Le Roy, Cukor, King Vidor, etc., as if there were any fundamental distinctions to personalize the single standardized style common to all of them, or about some good routine program film, as if it were a fresh, new, singular contribution to Film Art, flouting the formulae and conventions of popular entertainment. This practice is tantamount to writing profound critical essays about the "style" of Mary Roberts Rhinehart, Elinor Glyn, Rex Beach and Harold Bell Wright; yet it does not seem to disturb the film critics. Despite Vachel Lindsay and Gilbert Seldes, motion picture criticism has never succeeded in becoming a vital branch of American letters; but it seems to me on a lower level today than it was ten or even fifteen years ago.

In the last analysis, the whole issue comes down to this: putting aside the individual achievements of Griffith and the single masterpiece of Stroheim, the American cinema of the past two decades has made no fundamental progress. None of its advances, except along strictly mechanical lines, has been of real significance: none of the basic viewpoints of its practitioners toward the making of motion pictures has changed or progressed in any real sense. Twenty years after the capital American achievements in the realm of cinematic art—*Intolerance* and *The Birth of a Nation*—the Hollywood film-industry remains, as in the far-gone days of the nickelodeons, the foe of real art, the retarder of real cinematic progress—in short, the greatest single retroactive, anti-cultural influence in the world today. Projected in the light of a noble conception of Film Art, the best Hollywood products of our time are poor and contemptible things: in them there are no horizons, no imaginative heights, no passion, no ecstasy. Even in their "serious" moments, they are essentially trivial, ordinary, banal,—like the business-men who produce, direct and photograph them, and like the masses, who, hypnotized by Hollywood surface-finish, give the business-men ample reason to continue production along the same lines. In preparing a subject for the screen, every idea, every situation, has to be "adapted," *i.e.,* translated into the visual and dynamic terms of Film. But in Hollywood, this process of screen-adaptation means something else besides: It means the reduction of every story to the lowest level of human intelligence, the assimilation of every idea to the spirit and grain of the universal Average Man. This is merely another way of saying that Hollywood film-production automatically implies the suppression of creative imagination; the elimination of any and all possible moments of poetry in any given subject; and an enforced standardization of the style of the individual director, an obliteration of his temperament, to meet the requirements of popular taste. The outcome of this factory-process, through which every subject is put, may be, and frequently is, more charming, more "entertaining," than description of the process itself would indicate. But even at its best, the Hollywood product invariably emerges from the factory a negative quantity. A major agency of expression, it has neither enriched human life nor added one jot to the development of human consciousness. It has not presented a single fresh perspective of the world, nor projected a single significant vision of man and his destiny—(the one American effort in this direction, *Intolerance,* dates back two decades). In brief, except in the case of Griffith, the American screen has not contributed to the general enlightenment of the human race in any degree commensurate with its powers to do so. In place of this culture, it has offered what the movie-merchants call "sensational show values"—the half-truths, the superstitions, the vapid and sensual daydreams of the crowd.

It goes without saying that these severe strictures are, and have been, repeated *ad nauseum:* that they are sadly and brutally obvious. Certain alarming symptoms of contemporary film criticism, together with the increasing indifference to higher values of the more intelligent sections of the film-going public, necessitate a reiteration of the facts. The real danger is that the intelligent minority audiences, for want of better filmic nourishment, will come to reject anything better than the current movie fare of tinsel and candied pseudo-art. Then the prostitution of taste will be complete.

One question remains: What, if anything, can be done to regenerate this wayward behemoth, the American cinema? Any and all suggestions are apt to be feeble in view of the really formidable obstacles that beset the problem. In spite of the best possible remedies, the fact must not be lost sight of that control of the film industry proper is still vested in the present crowd and that the vacuous entertainment-film will continue to be produced in immense quantities for a long time to come. Nevertheless, one or two radical innovations should be obvious:

1. Above everything else, a university of the cinema, patterned after the one in Moscow but with emphasis on the formal and esthetic problems of the motion picture, should definitely be established here. It is a trifle absurd to consider that the Soviet Union, a new nation confronted with a thousand and one crucial problems involving its very survival as a society, should be the only country in the world today that can boast of an institution of film-culture, while in the United States, where the cinema as art received its original impetus, nothing exists except a few courses of doubtful value in "cinematography" in universities of Southern California and a highly commercialized course in "scenario writing" in a New York university. An American film university should be subsidized by the government in the interests of America's foremost art. The courses should be completely divorced from the exigencies of commercial film-production, and under no circumstances, save at the peril of the university's future, should a single magnate, executive, supervisor or producer from the Hollywood film industry be permitted to be a member of the board of trustees or perform any function whatever unless it be that of a voluntary benefactor. As a symbol of the university's educational direction and of its attitude toward Film as a cultural medium, a statue of Griffith should dominate the main foyer.

2. A Theatre of the Cinema should be established in at least every large city of the United States. Here the great films of all countries and of all periods should be pro-

jected in constant revivals. Each theatre should have a library of the cinema, consisting of well-preserved prints of old films and also of literature on the motion picture. To obviate the danger of control by ignorant distributors and petty racketeers, as happened with several of the film-arts guild organizations five or six years ago, all the theatres throughout the country should be controlled by a central theatre in New York City, in the same manner as the branches of a great metropolitan library. A nation-wide system of exhibition-centers of this nature would solve the distribution-problem for minority audiences who are fed up with the standard entertainment-product.

3. Entirely apart from the Theatre of the Cinema, the film-art movement itself should be revived. There should be a resurrection of film societies for purposes of discussion of the nature and destiny of the cinema, just as there are music clubs, Dickens societies, etc. The chief purpose of these clubs, however, will be to heighten interest in the exhibition of classics and experimental films at the theatres of the cinema. Through these organizations, thousands of new individuals will be attracted to Film Art. All the organizations together should issue a magazine, along the lines of *Experimental Cinema,* for the twofold purpose of making propaganda for the film-art movement and publishing critical and technical articles of value.

4. Independent creative film production should be subsidized by the government as the logical fruition of its support of the film university. The tragic exclusion from the industry of thousands of talented young men and women all over the country in favor of distinctly inferior and even degenerate talent, should give the Govern-

ment pause.—The money for these projects can be obtained by levying a culture-tax on all members of the Hollywood film industry receiving salaries of $100 a week and over.

5. A nation-wide campaign should be organized, using the screen itself as the principal instrument of propaganda, against censorship of the motion picture by the Church and the censor boards. The American film will never become a mature art-form until its champions succeed in freeing it from these ancient pests. Until this is done, it will be useless further to discuss the question of "what is wrong with the movies."

A concluding word: I am fully aware that this program for the regeneration of the American screen is hopelessly ideal and that it has not one chance in a million of being realized here for at least a century to come. I offer it, nevertheless, because only in this light can we see what is wrong with and about our greatest art. The practical solutions of practical men have all inevitably failed: they have been concerned with immediate stop-gaps and surface-reforms, not with fundamental changes that really change. As with society itself, so with the motion picture, the "practical" minds are the impractical ones; the shortest, easiest solution is the longest, hardest solution. One Griffith is worth the whole tribe of movie magnates; one *Intolerance* is worth all the "good" films Hollywood has ever made. This is merely another way of saying that the only final remedy for whatever ails any medium of human expression is a *creative* remedy, not a moral nor a social nor a political remedy. When this idea is fully understood by those who wish to "revolutionize" the movie in this country, a real revolution will be possible; then, and not before then, will the cinema become the glory, instead of the pointless joke, of American civilization.

CHAPTER XII

THE POET'S ATTITUDE TOWARD THE MOVIES
by

GABRIELA MISTRAL
(LUCILA GODOY)

(Translated from the Spanish by Marion A. Zeitlin)

THE poet's attitude toward the movies is necessarily the same as that which he adopts toward all things; he demands of the movies that the reality of the world be reduced, translated, wrought by them into poetry. Even though it may sound strange, this demand is most natural.

For who is the poet but that one for whom poetry constitutes both the true outward semblance of things and creatures and their inmost heart? The poet, with the same voice as the mystic, names as appearance, phantasmagoria, chaff and dross, all the material, heaped up or scattered abroad in the world, which has not yet been exalted to, or has ceased to be, poetry.

NATURALISM
The invention of the moving picture caused the *Naturalist* or *Realist* hosts to leap with joy. With it the reign of the image was being stoutly inaugurated: we were coming to a kind of *Transfiguration* of photography; an art was making its appearance that could have no other support than matter.

This time, as ever, the rational Demon was wrong, and the advantage slipped out of his hands and into those of the gods.

Naturalism (we take that of Zola as the archetype) is a puny undertaking, a march that exhausts itself after a few steps. Never has there been a school that wore itself out more easily, that spent itself more rapidly. A school is, in a way, like maternity: its virtue resides in its being fertile and its being able to overspread several centuries with its descendants. But naturalism proved sadly lacking in maternity; within fifty years its generative powers were gone.

Before thirty years had passed, it became evident that naturalism had succeeded only in making odious that which the Master considered to be Nature, but which was in reality no more than the outer integument of the natural, and was projecting the soul again and with meteor-like violence in the direction of the most unbridled poetry. Nature had acted somewhat like a vaccine against itself.

The cinema has turned out to be an art that evolves more rapidly than any other, the livest branch on the good tree of the Arts, an art directed, even in its worst zones, by people of greater talent than literary patrons. This may be seen in the fact that the return to fancy has been much more rapid in the movies than in literature.

IMAGINATION

I believe in the future of the cinema as great art only in proportion as it packs itself with imagination, and I should believe in its vertical decline if I saw in it the symptoms (ever arteriosclerotic) of slavery to the fact, to the phenomenon, to immediate reality.

I am using the word *reality* here not with the meaning that I myself give it, but with that given it by people in general. Reality for me is all they hold it to be, plus all the unseen worlds with which reality is inextricably interlocked.

Let us consider the landscape, which should afford the naturalist his greatest success. I have just seen a short and very felicitous French film, built on the theme of *water,* which if one were to judge by the announcements, promises something like an elementary chapter in realism.

The most beautiful—and most real—parts of this film are those in which a horizontal—or a vertical—mass of free water takes on fantastic aspects, ceasing to be water and coming to suggest some other element.

I recall certain mountain scenes where those spots and those moments were sought in which the mere mountain, released from itself, was transformed into a phantasmagoria of mirrors or into a misty dreamland.

Man—poor Zola never understood—is surfeited with man, satiated and nauseated with man. And it seems that, like us, what we call Nature and believe to be the rational *par excellence,* loathes being only what it is, and is ever seeking modes and attitudes which free it from its rusty hinges and send it flying down heroically mad ways.

The other perfectly rational domain which the movies invaded, besides the landscape, was that of biography or historical fact. At first sight, it seems that here as well, it would be impossible to escape the exact, the veracious; that here too, the *genre* would give more and more pleasure to the spectator in the degree that it conformed with the arid truth. Nothing of the kind: the Napoleons, Ivan the Terribles, Mary Stuarts, seen through the eyes of the historian, presented in schoolmaster fashion, were flat, tedious, stupid, in short, the very opposite of what those splendid figures really were. Then there began to appear Napoleons and Marys transformed into phosphorescent myths, fashioned by truth and dreaming in collaboration. The public, that seems so stupid, but is, in truth, like the child, who is never stupid—the public found a source of admiration and delight in those characters conceived in a cross-breeding of historical exactitude and beautiful fiction.

We shall go further yet in the future and weave our heroes of flesh and blood into the same tapestry of imagination and light as our *Parsifals* and *Lohengrins*.

Let us pass to another branch, in which the real is, to all appearances, triumphant: the scientific film, applied to botany, biology, or mineralogy.

We have seen the opening of a flower and its fertilization, witnessing the vegetable rite, an unadorned act of plant life; we have sliced away the disfiguring commentary and the auxiliary paraphernalia.

The flower, magnified so as to be enormously visible, is from the outset a very different flower from the one we knew; the stamens and pistil have become a forest; the calyx has been transformed into a kind of Roman fountain. The image takes hold of us, jolts us, carries us away, because of its metamorphosis, because it has ceased to be natural and has become fantastic. The same thing happens with the tissue of the human body, in which we are shown the circulation of the blood. We had never seen, nor even imagined, the wonder of the coursing of that mechanical and cunning fluid, which, at this very moment, is taking place within us; and when it is revealed to us in all its complexity, it all at once ceases to be looked upon by us as a natural (and, therefore, ordinary) function, and changes into wonder—that is, into food for the imagination rather than for the intellect.

What has been said applies equally well to the study of insects or the reactions of substances in a chemical experiment.

It still remains for us to cast a glance at the most fascinating portion of the movies of the past or the future: the juvenile movie. Let us make it clear that in using the word "juvenile," we have in mind the child, and not a certain moral zone which takes in all of us.

Without pretending to greatness—on the contrary, unconscious of being anything more than insignificant trifles—there appeared years ago, for the delight of children the whole series of "Mickies," "Felixes" and "Betty Boops." Prior to that, two other ways had been tried: that of the clown of flesh and blood, and that of the simple puppet or marionette. The clown wore out quickly: he lacked the piquant aid of verbal buffoonery, and without his jests, soon palled. The puppets made a much greater contribution, so much so that it may be said that the clever animated cartoon of today is another puppet show, conceived and made for children, and proving to be excellent for the adult seeker after carnal—and angelical—laughter.

I expressly say *angelical* to indicate a *genre* which is

on the way, but has not yet arrived. Juvenile humor is being elaborated gradually from a curious mixture of the adult, the infantile, the zoological and the angelical. Time and space make it impossible for me to describe completely this attractive field with its interplay of mischievous, grotesque and beautiful elements. This simple indication is sufficient for anyone familiar with the subject.

GREAT THEMES

If motion-picture publications failed to signalize Wells' "The Invisible Man" as one of the successes of the year, it must have been because no great stars took part in this film, and because so worthwhile a work as this was not approached with all the emphasis on complete realization that it deserved.

Nevertheless, in spite of having been made with second-rate actors and with a niggardly outlay of money, this film, belonging to the imaginative type, pleased the crowd, and at the same time, afforded the cultivated a glimpse of the possibilities of the fantastic movie.

Here lies a dangerous fault in the moving-picture industry. With the exception of Germany, Russia, and, occasionally, the United States, the general rule is for it to spend large sums on silly stories, which are finally put over by means of great actors and outrageous extravagance in the settings.

On the other hand, it adopts masterly stories infrequently, intrusts them to mediocre actors, and expends money grudgingly for their production.

I shudder at the thought of someday seeing "The Divine

Comedy" acted by bunglers with wretched pasteboard sets to represent Heaven and Hell; or "Hamlet," put on by gesticulating puppets and mumbling ghosts.

The masterpiece has not yet been given financial support in keeping with its dignity by an industry which stands today among the most opulent. Such works are either eliminated because they are still regarded as bogies terrible to face, or else they are produced by the overbold in a style that reminds one of the way they are presented in small towns in the tableaux of school children—that is, with the most beautiful of cynicism.

THE GENERAL PUBLIC AND FANCY

It is unbelievable how the people, generally looked upon as the Sancho Panza *par excellence,* a creature of sight, hearing and touch, a Herod that abhors and persecutes the creations of the imagination—it is unbelievable, I say, how they love imagination above the best reality, how they seek after it if the way is opened to them, and how, once they are in its realm, they are allured by it, partake of it, revel in it, and are loath to give it up.

Absurd though it may seem, it is the most natural thing in the world. Those masses of industrial workers and small functionaries lived imagination—if ever—in their first seven years. Afterwards, work cast them headlong into the blackest slime, into the foulest cloacas of the real. Here they vaguely long for the phosphorescence with which things glowed when they looked at them or touched them as children; each one dimly retains in his thoughts the memory of the man he was before becoming merely a stevedore, miner or garbage collector—that is, the memory of the child, the angel that consumes and produces wonder.

Neither the musician nor the poet went near this man, degraded by the "nobility" of labor and turned by it into the reverse of what he really is. It was necessary for the movies and the radio to come for poet, painter and musician to enter his life and reinstill all the old, holy illusions without which none of God's creatures can remain what he was intended to be.

I realize very well that through these two sluices, the radio and the movies, open now and forever upon the masses, there has poured forth also all the great stupidity, the tacky shoddiness, the crudity of poor art which plebeianizes as much as good art ennobles. But, at any rate, these sluices allow nobility to pass out along with the scum and the mud, and he who understands, little by little learns to separate them, tastes spirituality, and is saved.

It seems that there were no other channels than these dangerous ones of the radio and the movies through which art might flow out abundantly over popular life. We must accept them and be thankful for them, therefore, without wavering as we musicians and writers have in the past.

Each new discovery becomes a sort of autonomous being, and has, like us, its demons and its angels who attend it in legions, just as they did the Jew of the Zohar. Each invention scarcely sees the light when it must, like Adam, set about defending itself from those Satanical parasites which fall upon it as soon as it begins to grow, and seek to live on it and devour it, or to attach themselves to it.

Among the demons of the movies let us count *Realism;* and let us point to *Poetry* as its good genius.

For the first time since what is called "popular education" has existed, there might now be a chance to elevate the masses through the imaginative. The schools have *handled* the masses through the will and through the emotions—in a much smaller way, through the intellect —using pedagogies that resolve themselves into little more than emotive, volitive and intellectual hocus-pocus.

The imagination, an aristocratic faculty if there ever was one, and the oldest of all, being the mother of two of those mentioned, has never constituted a serious interest, much less an acknowledged aim of any well-known pedagogy—inasmuch as the pedagogical leader is commonly the man most lacking in it that ever God set loose upon the earth.

The movies might take over this untouched field in popular education, that is, imagination on a huge scale, which is viewed with horror by incapable pedagogues and completely neglected by stupid parents.

REPROACHES

Three classes of well-intentioned people cry out against the movies from the four points of the compass: teachers, clergymen, and parents. The first want, more or less, a utilitarian cinema that would help them teach lessons— or replace them—and that would calm down the rather tragic tumult they have brought to the child's mind. The second want films that will not pervert the devout clientele

of their churches, and that will aid, if possible, their soul-
saving sermons. The third demand of the movies that
they shall not go on inciting their children to lives of
adventure with detective stories, gangsters, gypsies, etc.

Teachers may be answered by saying that the moving
picture will be vertically educational only within the
boundaries of the school, and that in Rome a certain
International Educational Cinematographic Institute, to
which they attach little importance, is engaged, under the
auspices of the League of Nations, in supplying better
and better—at times even perfect—material. But the
extra-scholastic movie, the commercial spectacle, can
never become more than obliquely educational, because
children seek it as pure pleasure, as they seek water for
their boats or wind for their kites.

To clergymen, it may be said that the struggle between
church and cinema for the soul of the hearer and spectator
is going to be won, not by the purer (alas!), but by the
better judge of human nature, by the one that offers the
more savory bait to the terrible prey, which is very
worldly and demands, even of the Gospel, an insnaring
eloquence.

The answer to parents is that they have so neglected to
make their children read, to give them noble adventure
in books and, more especially, in the nursery tale, in
short, that they have been and are parents so Mosaic in
their imperious dryness and doctrinal wearisomeness, that
their very vital offspring have slipped away from them
and tumbled over the precipice of the gangster film. Let
them learn entrancingly to tell and repeat Homer or
Shakespeare, let them become capable of gay puerilities,

and it is possible that as in the mystery of homeopathy, they may cure the hopeless cancer with the white aconite of the bedtime story about dragons and goblins, which they have so long been omitting to tell.

The poet, at this point, can give his solemn assurance that imagination, great imagination, saves here too, and that it is moral for the very reason that it is not professionally so. The imagination, like things universally, has its underground cellars and its sunny chambers, and he who has not grown accustomed to live in the sunlight of balcony and terrace, must live among the musty odors of the basement, at home with bats and dampness. Great imagination, which is of starry essence, which is itself a firmament, does not vitiate palates, pollute bodies or communicate noxious fevers. Vitiation and fever are the portion of that gentleman so dear to the good *bourgeois,* who has gone by the name of *Naturalism.*

THE POET'S PLEA AND DEMAND

We poets ask of the movies this thing which we have given up asking of the school because we are completely disillusioned with it. We must have at least as much right to be heard on this question as the Salvation Army has to demand sickly moralities, or Manufacturers' Associations to call for something that will "pep up" labor.

What we demand has already been indicated: that they should reproduce a state of childhood in the adult and prolong it in the child by means of the story of pure imagination; that they should, with the instrument of fancy, rejuvenate this world which goes limping along like a cripple with its broken limbs and its noble passions all awry. The theologians, exalted gentlemen, say of imagination that she gave birth to the world, God's imagining, and that since that divine phantasmagoria nothing tonic has ever happened in history that has not been brought forth by her, the one and only cause of miracles in this world.

CHAPTER XIII

A THEATRICAL PRODUCER'S REACTION
TO THE MOVIES

by

BROCK PEMBERTON

ANY number of producers might have been invited by the editor of this symposium who would have contributed a more intelligent and enlightened opinion than your deponent, but in all modesty I question whether any could have been found with a more definite and biased viewpoint. I don't like motion pictures. And I'll tell you why.

As far as I have been able to determine I was the world's first movie critic. In 1915 I was assistant dramatic editor and critic of the New York Times. I was on space, which translated means, I was paid for anything I wrote that was published at so much per column, and to add to my income I appointed myself movie critic. Since I was self-appointed I have only myself to blame. The Times was always a pleasant, easy-going, gentlemanly sheet; and so while no one in authority had suggested that I become its motion-picture critic, none told me to desist. Every Sunday for a year or more I ruined my week-ends by seeing two or three photoplays, or feature pictures, as the designation ran in those days, and by attempting to piece together a readable column about them. Readable or otherwise, I was paid twelve dollars a column and in those days twelve dollars was a hundred dollars New Deal Money.

But the experience left its mark. It did something terrible to me. If I had become a father at that period I'm sure my children would have been not acrobats but silent picture actors with celluloid collars. For years I invariably crossed the street to avoid passing in front of a motion-picture cathedral and until the advent of talking pictures I rarely ever entered one again. My aversion was so great that I even missed the good ones, films like "The Birth of A Nation" and the Chaplin comedies, though occasionally in holiday mood abroad I was able to face some of these.

I am quite willing to admit that my inability to cherish the cinema was due to a deficiency in me. After the original amusement furnished by the novelty of animated pictures had worn off movies began definitely to irk me. They were still in their infancy—the phrase has a familiar ring—when I nominated myself critic, although they had been graduated from the nickelodeon era of unrelated shots to the poisonous period of the photoplay. As the pictures progressed from rags to riches, the theatres in which they were projected evolved from planks to plush, and as both took on opulence it seemed to me the stupidities of the movies increased directly with the number of reels, till the six-reeler became six times as deadly as a one-reeler.

As regards the cinema there are two definite types of mind, the one adjusted to their technique, the other maladjusted. A pleasurable reaction is the reward of the former, an irritable one the latter. Without cultivating a pose I had the misfortune to be born with a mind out of gear with the cinema. I remember once writing an article for Jacob Wilk, then a literary agent, the theme of which was that the motion picture was a bastard art in that it did not attempt to tell a story exclusively through the medium of pictures but resorted to the use of words. The perfect silent picture, I wrote, would be one in which no printed caption or title appeared. Ironically, the same Mr. Wilk, now a movie executive, was instrumental twenty years later in effecting my first tieup with a picture company. It was not till the end of the silent era, just before Warner Brothers said "Let there be sound," to borrow a phrase from one of my current productions, that the ideal of my unpublished soliloquy, the title-less photoplay, appeared on the scene. It was a German importation, and it created a sensation as it should have because it was a fine picture.

But the pardon came too late. I think it was the titles, of all the photoplay's idiocies, that enraged me most. Remember the titles? Those printed, descriptive absurdities that crowded the pictures off the screen at all-too-frequent intervals? From illiteracy they ascended to whimsy-whamsy, reaching their apogee in the classic, "Came The Dawn." They were almost easier to take before they became refined, but ungrammatical or literate they always irritated me. While my mind was not attuned to receiving a story through the medium of pictures the intermittent interruptions of printed legends were more maddening. They were invariably reflected long enough to permit the most complete moron a chance to read them through, so that if one were only ordinarily stupid, possessing the traditional audience-mind of a child of twelve, one could re-read the jewel several times, and when through take up parsing or knitting.

Then there was the childishness of the material. Aimed at the heads of the twelve-year-old audience-intellect the aim was so poor the stories hit the region of the collective appendix. In retrospect silent pictures may loom as classics. I saw some recently on an ocean-liner. The captain thought there was a storm, the boat rocked so from our laughter.

The taste displayed was generally atrocious, especially the visual taste, and since the appeal was wholly to the eye this lack was devastating. The interior decorations of American homes undoubtedly received an artistic set-back from the films it hasn't yet recovered from. The average "interior" looked like nothing so much as a window display in an Eighth Avenue installment furniture house.

And then there were the players themselves, the majority strange personalities of every nationality who through tricks of fate or personality became the adored of the world. A few of them were real, the mass were nonentities whom fly-blown fame made even more vapid. This, more than all other monstrous circumstances surrounding the silent flickers, enraged me. That persons so devoid of all qualities considered necessary for success should be both successful and popular convinced me that John Barrymore's extemporaneous curtain-line on the occasion of an off-key laugh was well taken. "Better death," gritted John through grinding teeth on the occasion of rude laughter as he lay prostrate on the floor in his death struggle at the end of a performance of "Redemption," "than to have to live in this world with a lot of — — — fools."

Beginning as improbable persons, many of them became impossible as fame and wealth swamped them, till toward the end of the regime Hollywood rivalled the Augean stables.

CAME THE DAWN! Toward the end of the silent picture era the vast industry—the seventh, or am I thinking of a Commandment?—started to skid. Even the American public, bulwark of the cinema audience, began to weary of the same story retold in new costumes. In addition to flossing up the reels with comic titles, musical scores had been added and the customers novocained into insensibility with pipe-organ or orchestral obligatos of original or classical scores. This anaesthetic prolonged life for a period but soon exhibitors discovered that while their seats were full their cash registers were empty. Business engineers solved the riddle—the customers came for the first show and slept through the others! Or, if they didn't sleep, they didn't rely solely on the screen for entertainment.

These became the Old Guards of the Silents who, after the Warners uttered their famous ukase, bemoaned the passing of all that was beautiful. Some were no doubt sincere, though I question whether they would stick to their story if they could see one of their old flickers today. Whenever they are shown as curiosities on modern programs shrieks of mirth escape the customers.

The real resistance to the new order came from Hollywood itself. Few, at the first raspings and croakings, realized an era had passed and a new one had begun. Most of the mimes couldn't manage understandable let alone cultured speech, so they wanted no part of the novelty. The stylized pantomime that passed for action and reaction to emotion bore no relation to life and the expression of emotion through words. Likewise the directors knew the accepted tricks of their trade but nothing of the new technique and were loud in their protests that sound was a passing fad. In the counting houses there was still a balance on the right side of the ledger and the purveyors to the nickelodeons who had grown up to be the Titans of the World's Seventh Largest Industry preferred to fight it out along the old lines.

In spite of this opposition, many in all classes were swept into oblivion as the sound engineers rapidly perfected their mechanisms. More of the business Titans were able to make the leap than were the players and directors, for after all, business is business while art is art.

I still don't like motion pictures; but I don't dislike talkies as I did silent films. Talkies at least approximate the spoken drama which, to borrow another phrase from my favorite current comedy, "is my life." I spend so many of my evenings going down the aisles to watch bad plays I haven't much time to devote to bad pictures. I know most of them are bad because I go to some of the best.

Only those who write plays know better than we who produce them what a difficult job it is to present a good one to the public. The movie makers at last understand the seriousness of our problem, for talkies are condensed plays. Camera tricks may help, but unless there is a dramatic story under the tramping feet, the whizzing clock hands, the falling calendar leaves, the tricks are empty. The novelty of sound with pictures carried them for a year or two. Then the army demanded merit, and now, unless merit is awarded, the army deserts.

This audience insurrection resulted in probably the most striking feature of the revolution. Any silent film however febrile earned its investment and usually a handsome profit. Likewise its cost was comparatively low, except for the spectacles. Any talking picture may lose hundreds of thousands of dollars, and many of them do. When sound was attached to the screen Hollywood was forced into show business. Till then it had been concerned with a manufacturing business.

The mimes and directors of the silent films fought for a year or two but only a few made the grade. Some of the great names of yesterday are in the lists of extras today. For while the entrepreneurs were discovering that although a simple tale patched up with illiterate titles might mug itself into prosperity the same story spoken could not be illiterate. The actors were likewise finding out to their sorrow that the expression of emotion through facial contortions and bodily writhings was one thing and through the spoken word quite another. Also the technique of building a story was different.

So in spite of all the prophets of doom, who through self-interest or conservatism squawked, the old order disappeared and in the places of the false prophets came hundreds of men and women from the theatre of flesh and blood.

There followed another great change. At first the physically beautiful, both men and women, were the only ones to succeed. Soon the audience discovered that visual beauty is only a part of it and men and women of character and personality, sometimes actually forbidding in appearance, crowded out the baby dolls and patent-leather crowned he-vamps.

At the moment the spoils are about evenly divided, the rugged personalities who can really act on one side, the cute, pretty and handsome who can perform just enough to get by on the other. Fortunately for the multitude who must subsist on canned drama the screen requires precious little acting ability. The camera enlarges everything to such a degree that the faintest show of emotion is effective on the screen. The duration of any scene in shooting is rarely more than a minute or two, and the weakest itsy-bitsy ingenue can work up strength enough for this period. If the scene isn't right it is shot over and over till the director is satisfied or the "rushes" show his idea of perfection has been reached.

How different the legitimate stage where a scene may be a full act in building and the actor's power of co-ordination is taxed every second. The hardest lesson the experienced stage player has to learn when he faces the camera and microphone is to minimize his powers.

I stated this slight histrionic demand of the screen on the actor is fortunate for the public because beauty in any form is to be desired, and if a player is not endowed with both beauty of character and physical beauty it is something to have the latter. In the words of the old adage, half a "loafer" is better than none.

The introduction of sound, then, has removed many of my hates from pictures. The stories are superior to those of silent days and the personnel has changed almost completely. A great many actors whom I gave their first parts are among the screen's brightest stars, dozens of others who have acted or written plays for me are doing their bit in Hollywood, while I have passing acquaintance with scores of others. As far as those who are making pictures are concerned I would feel almost as much at home in Beverly Hills as I do on Broadway. I have respect for most of Hollywood now whereas previously I held a vast part of it in contempt.

What, then, is my grouch? I have none, really, against the talkies themselves though I could debate with their makers. If I were marooned in an inland town as I was in my youth, cut off from the better things of the theatre or perhaps from it altogether, I would no doubt be a cinema addict. I don't like second-rate theatre, so why should I care for second-rate cinema? As a part of my business I have to see many plays. I could witness a good one every night and never tire, but unfortunately only about one-tenth that number are written. If the play looks promising I attend the first performance in order to form my opinion without benefit of critics. This has won me a medal in one of those "ten most" nominations as the most ubiquitous first-nighter, a dubious distinction but the best I can boast after fifteen years of producing, till another comes along.

The principal disadvantage springing from this exalted position is that I witness many inferior offerings. Since I know from the reviews, their titles and those involved in their making that most pictures are inferior why should I bother? I don't.

I do not worry about the cinema as a competitor. Economic conditions, and our own short-sighted policy as managers of sending inferior attractions on tour, are responsible for the disappearance of the "road." If we had the plays and players we could compete with the movies, even retaining our high price scales, in any town in the country. With the world a financial shambles naturally the cheaper form of entertainment has the edge. But the thing that prevents most of us from being Napoleons of the drama is pressing the movie barons, as it is us, closer to the wall, a lack of first-rate material. In an uncomfortably short time after the introduction of sound the public became captious. As the standard of the product rose, so did the public's critical standards. The manufacturer of a program of fifty to sixty films a year is more to be pitied than censured. Two plays a year is my average and half of them don't live up to expectations.

One of the topics I would debate would be the short-sighted policy of Hollywood toward the theatre. A census of screen talent would show that the vast bulk of it was stage-trained, and yet, instead of looking on the theatre as an ally, a training school on which they must depend for their future supply of talent, many of the picture makers treat it as a deadly rival. No sooner do we discover new talent than Hollywood abducts it. Our premieres are peopled with scouts, while even the tryout performances and the Summer theatres are policed. I never open a play without placing the actors, whose removal I feel would be a serious loss, under run-of-the-play contracts.

What makes this raiding policy particularly maddening is that the picture cohorts seem to have no judgement of their own. If they read in the newspapers that an actor or author is good they immediately try to sell him down the river at a fancy salary, whereas they probably have snubbed the same individual when his or her services were offered before the New York press bestowed its approval. This is a daily happening.

If the importuned one succumbs the chances of those on the lot knowing how to utilize the new talent are negligible. Two incidents that followed my production of "Personal Appearance" this season are typical. The script was shown to many movie companies in advance of production without any of them becoming excited about it or the author, Lawrence Riley. The play received a fine press and immediately young Mr. Riley was besieged with offers and finally whisked off to the Coast at a staggering salary. Although "Personal Appearance" was the season's comedy hit, Mr. Riley was immediately assigned to work on a tragedy.

A stock leading woman hitherto unknown to New York appeared in two small comedy parts last season. After the first appearance a picture company made a test of her, passed their option, and following her second role another company placed her under contract. Some months later I borrowed the young woman from the contracting company and in the role of a movie siren on a tour of personal appearance she became an over-night sensation in Mr. Riley's comedy. Our heroine was none other than Gladys George, and while Miss George undoubtedly can play emotional and tragic roles, being an actress schooled in the best stock companies, it was as a comedienne that the movie scouts and I saw her. And yet her first Hollywood assignment was in a drab little item in which she portrayed a humorless, gunman's moll, while the one they were contemplating handing her when I interrupted was that of a nun! Something must be wrong with a system as cockeyed.

One thing wrong is that Hollywood is too remote from New York—its main source of supply for scripts, actors and directors. Those continually on the lot grow provincial, a state of mind not relieved by a tendency to become ingrown which afflicts the whole community. There is a possibility that this insularity will shortly be corrected by the removal of the industry from Hollywood. Only the vast property investment has kept it there since the demise of silent pictures, which needed California's eternal sunlight. This is no longer a factor with talkies photographed almost exclusively within doors. Threatened high taxes and the constant menace of recurring earthquakes may drive the studios eastward. Their next stop will surely be nearer Manhattan, perhaps in New Jersey. That near any one should be able to tell the difference between a hawk and a handsaw.

A consummation as to the stage and screen devoutly wished, by me at least, seems about to be realized. I have always preached that the two mediums, instead of battling one another, should coöperate to the fullest degree. Movie companies have sporadically invested in stage productions generally with disastrous results, due to faulty setups. At the moment some of the larger companies have arranged or are negotiating to become associated with leading New York producers in the production of plays. A common interest will draw the two camps more closely together and each will be benefited. The exchange of players between stage and screen, already on the increase, will then be the usual procedure. This will revitalize the player, lengthen his period of popularity and heighten interest in both mediums. The greater financial and exploitation resources of the cinema will restore the "road."

I again borrow the words of Mr. Shakespeare and say that this is a consummation devoutly to be wished. If it does not come to pass within the next few years mark me down as a poor prophet.

CHAPTER XIV

THE MOVIES AND THE SOCIAL REVOLUTION

by

WOLF W. MOSS

FLAGRANT irresponsibility furnishes the reason for the production of movies singularly removed from the actual facts of the day. By encouraging this escape-medium the producers have invalided the normal development of mind, arrested the powers of discrimination by subversive half-truths, thwarted and dwarfed every creative instinct by forced and devitalizing attempts to create a beautiful mirage, thus distracting our attention from conditions that have their roots in the embittered definite forces of hunger, poverty, physical and mental humiliation. The level of man being forcibly maintained much lower than we truthfully care to admit, it becomes relatively simple to continue his subjugation by unreal flossy and insipid pictures.

It is this basis that the producers use as their guide for audience reaction. They are notorious for satisfying the cravings of the mass populations of the world no matter what the locale or the folklore may be, or the inability of the many nations to assimilate, or even begin to understand, the vagaries of the screen's portrayals. In other words, the world audiences do not understand that what they are paying for the pleasure of seeing, was created only after they had been considered. It is, of course, true that success must crown as many pictures as possible, otherwise the medium that now gives you such genuine pleasure, relaxation and thought could not continue and you, the audience, would be the tragic loser. I might add at this point that so interested have all picture magnates been as to audience reaction throughout the world that it is doubtful whether five articles have been written on the subject in the last five years by their research departments.

Movies are the battering-ram in the world today. They run rough-shod over all forms of culture, destroying the philosophic concepts developed through ages, ignoring the folklore, the native traditions, violating and vitiating with mad abandon all that stands in their path, for they recognize nothing but themselves, their own transgressing powers.

With the introduction of the movies into China, accessible although they were to less than one-fifth of the population, they at once became the main educational force of western civilization and culture. Containing great sexual freedom and attempting multiferous variations on the theme of the triangle, they have to be credited for markedly altering the social relationship of the sexes. The liberty of choice in marriage, heretofore made for countless generations in family councils, is being abandoned by the younger generation for love matches. Youth strongly demanded its own control. Special note may be called toward feminine unbound feet, but in this field the missionaries are deserving of praise.

Of far reaching importance is the fact that when

movies come to the technically backward countries only the richer elements can afford the expense of buying tickets. For their superficial pleasures they witness luxuries in as mad an abandon as their far-fetched dreams. But as one rich class watches the caprice of another affluent group, there is created a common bond between them that instinctively retroacts as entrenchments of greater imagined superiority over the balance of their countrymen, thereby separating them more than ever from the grim realities and great problems of their country. As for the other four-fifths of the population who cannot afford to go to the movies, and who are therefore beyond the pale of recognition as human beings, they are overlooked—forgotten in their rice fields, tea fields, mud huts, forgotten among their horrible ravaging diseases, among the famines and floods, as are the workers in the country in which the pictures are produced— forgotten slaves in the shops, the mills and in factory owned properties.

Sweeping through the world with this medium of audience-reaction, we encounter strikingly similar sociological upheavals with the advent of the movies. No matter where they are shown they exhibit total unconcern with the ideology of their audiences. They are primarily concerned with, and are more strongly interested in, today, during depression, discovering what type of entertainment the people would most gladly pay for and would most likely return to see again in slightly altered form. In some countries, such as India and China, audiences express their distaste by loudly hissing the picture, not once, but will return four or five times to show their evident disapproval. If greater percentages of the audiences could be induced to return three or four times to show their distaste, it follows every probability that the box office smashes of the day would be made with an eye toward consumer opprobrium, no matter how bad those pictures would be. Upon this basis lies the producers' knowledge of audiences, and upon the basis of gross receipts does he judge the success of his particular brand of exhibition.

Let us pause for one moment to watch the release of a picture. It is given advance press notices in all parts of the world, and is rushed by fastest carriers to destinations for showing. Whether in Bombay or Sidney, Malay or Toronto, Yokohama or Buenos Aires, Zanzibar or Paris, it is made clear to you that this new movie is a triumph far exceeding in general excellence the film at which you are now looking. But what great authority, what great understanding force is there in Hollywood that is able to reduce to a single consumer's unit the audiences of the world as to assume that no matter what is filmed has universal appeal?

The religious attendance to motion pictures the world over comes from the desire of men and women to find escape from the daily drudgeries, from their drab, colorless lives. Year after year greater percentages of the world's people must of necessity turn to them. Faced with tremendous complexities, equipped with no education or an illusionary one, they find it impossible to rationalize the processes of their lives. Sensitively created, they are subjugated and beaten at every step they take. They can achieve no orderliness, no security, being always prey to economic variations that simply use them in greater or smaller quantities. From birth they have only so much use-value as workers and this is soaked from them in as short a period as possible, with husks of men remaining, and with them the husks of a capitalist civilization.

For a few brief moments submerged in darkened picture palaces they sink beneath the sedatives into blissful forgetfulness. Thwarted, never able to express their own emotions fully, they borrow for a period, travel and beauty, love and romance, sympathy and compassion, imagination and solace from the flashing panoramas that unfold as if in promised hope for them. And so day after day they come back to feed upon this false stimulus. They become satisfied. Life is made tolerable.

Of greatest tragedy remains the discussions involved about the problems of the mirage-people. Minutely their sadness and triumph are shared, and giving them consideration are those who never have had any consideration in return. Home from the movies, every move and inflection is discussed and thrashed out as if they were great vital problems. The serfs assist the king. So real do these lives become, so miserable and despairing are their own lives, that in the imaginings of bewildered people they begin to assume the shapes, actions and thoughts of their imagined counterparts. These they defend with true heroism.

And all the time never so much as a mention that dire want faces the world because greed, thievery and falseness have made the world an economic battlefield with profits as the only objective. In one hands lies the tremendous power of reaching the whole world, and the finest propaganda medium in defense of the privileged class. But this power, great as it is, becomes gargantuan when it is seen that this same band controls the radio and television.

Is it therefore any wonder that motion-picture producers never show or even intimate that poverty and subsistence levels are the part of approximately seventy-five per cent of the world's population? Entertainment they claim, cannot be social propaganda, yet they did not hesitate in deliberately manufacturing anti-Sinclair propaganda in the studios and presenting them to the state of California as authentic newsreels. But this thing they call entertainment, what is it? As best expressed it is a thing that runs in cycles, similar to depressions, with the present era of censorship recreating the sweet and light motif. If a picture featuring gangsters and killings proves successful, then the public wants it, and the cycle begins. And so impotent do our best writers and directors become when reaching Hollywood that no matter what they do or say, they must fit the pattern or be forgotten.

The story of Eisenstein is an excellent example and bears repeating. Invited to come to Hollywood and guaranteed privileges in deference to his famous directorial skill, he was given a Jesuit-father story among the Indians in the Southwest, to adapt for the screen. Eisenstein was uninterested in this theme but prepared what was admitted a brilliant scenario on the story of "Sutter's Gold." This was rejected on the ground that it illustrated an unpalatable moral. He then undertook Theodore Dreiser's "American Tragedy," which he understood as Dreiser had meant it to be understood: that the trial was an indictment of the society which was condemning Clyde Griffiths and those standards he had tried to live up to. Again, the studio executives rejected the scenario, and were convinced of Eisenstein's unwillingness to conform to pattern of the world a la Hollywood.

The great art and knowledge of Eisenstein which these same executives had so admired and coveted when placed in their possession became valueless, due to their inability to use this same great skill with the freedom of expression that was its essential basis. Themselves compressed within definitely measured, inarticulate walls, the demand was that Mr. Eisenstein become as inanimate, as unresponsive toward human problems as they themselves are. This, Eisenstein could not do.

The movies also stand indicted for their meaningless and uninforming newsreels which are flashed on the screen to indicate world movements, news events of importance, the tempo of a changing world. Strictly censored or perverted is any news that might give the masses of the world an inkling that their earthly lot *can* be altered and that in almost all countries there are men and women courageous enough who are giving their lives to bring this about. Instead, here again, the opiate is applied, and the deeds of oppressors and knaves especially such as Mussolini, Hitler and their cohorts are made into the great thinkers and actionists of the day.

To gain markets, the movies claim to offer "International interest" entertainment and boast about their power of creating amity among men. But even though their distribution is world-wide, even though international in scope, yet at no time have they manifested this tendency. Not a single essence of the countries outside of their own, except possibly for settings alone, has been introduced authentically within the films. They use stereotyped characters established by a fascistic press: a Frenchman looks and acts so, a German so, a Russian so, a Chinaman so.

Recently Mr. Louis B. Mayer, head of MGM, in working for the defeat of a state tax bill made the statement that "heathens and foreigners were responsible for great sources of revenue that the state of California had no right to tax." When the head of a studio is so ignorant as to the importance of other nationalities that he can make degrading remarks about them with impunity, what can be expected from that studio that will indicate development beyond their cloistered temples?

As long as the movies are greatly controlled by the American producing companies, it remains difficult to judge them with productions in other countries. We can compare them with British films, but their development is recent and technically Hollywood remains without peer. But to further understand the future of the movies and their possibilities, it is necessary that a comparison be drawn with the theatre.

What is the condition of the theatre today? What are its possibilities for the future? What drama developments have taken place in the fascistic countries, and, for definite comparison, in Soviet Russia? What part does the audience play in the theatre that it cannot in the movies, and why will the theatre continue to be the leader of ideas which must flow to the movies as a secondary sequence?

The contemporary theatre is frustrated. In countries

like Spain, Sweden, Holland, Germany, and Italy, the theatre is either state-subsidized or movements are afoot to see that it becomes so shortly. Few managers wish to expend money attempting new dramatic forms. Stagnation results. This lack of possibility of production reduced the desire of young writers and of those who had talent coupled with ambition. All new strong dramatic forms are forbidden.

Thus we witness the peculiar phenomenon of the growth of a new generation without the possibility of expressing itself. It must remain tied to old and repetitive forms, simply because the theatre runs under a profit and loss system for a small clique of owners. Here again there is no regard for the audience. They are allowed the privilege of paying for transparent bedroom farces, idiotic sleuthing mysteries, etc. The progress that the theatre must make must be in the direction of mass expression. It can no longer remain aloof like an expensive plaything. It must be used for experimentation of new forms, it must be the laboratory through which is pictured, with skill and honesty, the ever changing forces of world movements. It cannot remain aloof. This aloofness has been responsible for its death.

Let us look at the Canadian theatre and at the recent financial assistance given to the little theatre movement by the Governor General. When the jubilation died even the reactionary members faintly perceived that this stimulus showed a lack of health, that essentially it rested on false grounds. A few more injections would not change the results. It was inevitable that it would not work because it had nothing to offer. Presentations depended entirely upon success shows, remuneratively, of course, from New York and London. The other great successes were of the old masters, to be had from French's and Dennison's. But what about Canada's own playwrights? What about Canada's own particular ideology, its own problems understandable to all Canadians? Why wasn't the only group that mattered really encouraged, instead of disregarded? The answer is the same the world over when private property and privileges and profits are assailed and when the primary rights of human beings are being fought for.

It is good to know that in Canada there is a theatre not dependent on patent medicine sources for drama, but one that takes root, in the lives, struggles and joys of the toilers in the shops, mines, farms and slave camps. This is the worker's theatre. Plays enacted are those written in the heat of life by these same workers. When six actors and a suitcase containing all the properties and costumes needed for seven plays pack themselves into a small roadster for a tour, they cannot depend very much on the elaborate fakery that has been built up by the capitalist stage to fool tired people into thinking and believing that they are seeing a real play. Audiences must be a part of the company of actors.

The success of an actor depends upon his collaboration with the audience. To be an accomplished artist is to be able to regulate this tempo of collaboration so that the theatre becomes a place of emotional display for audiences no less than actors. This direct force, this surcharged emanation of feelings that sensitively yet forcibly adds to the impetus of the role is lacking in viewing a photographed object. The screen does not, it cannot, achieve a true affinity of mood. The theatre will have to act as its feelers, groping, at present, blindly, for audience reaction.

The peoples of the world can be, after all, servile for only a certain period. It must be expected that higher intellectual levels will be reached; that workers the world over will be educating the people and that in the proportion that people are educated they will desert the movies for the theatre—the educational theatre that draws from their lives, that emanates their spirit, that shares their triumphs and bitter pains. At this junction, we will find, if still existing in present form, remarkable reasons being offered for falling attendances and even more remarkable remedies.

The part of the dramatic critics in the theatre has been to serve as the antennae, the critical and intellectual powerhouse. Primarily, they must be constructive forces. But to be constructive and to be an intelligent critic it is indispensable that interests remain keen and that these same interests be universal in scope. Continuous erudition is essential. It is the only pivot-point from which any critic has the right to speak with authority. The greater the critic's knowledge the more weight he carries.

Let us then review recent critic activities, and here I speak generally, admitting that there are a few who can be honored. For diagnosis it is best to take "The American Theatre as seen by its Critics," a recent symposium written by these same critics. What clearer condemnation can there be than that some of them have no idea whatsoever of the art that they respond to in particular, and no clear notion of what they desire it to be? They jumble along with their enthusiasms, acidities, theories and happy reminiscences with a certain irregularity and abandonment paralleling the theatre itself in its present vacillating state. The critics are by their own confessions reduced to an elemental part in the kaleidoscopic whole. Instead of direction-instruments, instead of educated powers with a true love for their art that would make of their criticisms a profound guide for future theatre development, they are merely theatre reporters interested in the privileges that are their due. It would appear that after a certain number of years of theatre reporting, all critics become geniuses, all become infallible at charming tea discussions and all add materially to the success of the pulps whose advertisers keep these pulps going.

The motion-picture critic's job is easier, much easier. All he has to do is put a few stars after pictures. Even children understand their splendid significance, and children are a valuable box-office asset. Overlooked is the fact that these stars could have been in colors, baby pink and baby blue; or if this is negatively regarded, why not silver and gold stars? After all, a four-star-picture might deserve only a silver rating and not a gold star. Or in accompaniment to the military consciousness now being stirred, why not be patriotic and use gold stripes? Or would these suggestions which I offer gratis involve too many additional headaches for the now overworked cinema critics?

Like many other people I am interested in knowing how a movie reviewer can be called a critic. While the theatre critic upon occasion has some technical knowledge, the movie critic has little or none at all. To all intents and purposes he is merely an advance drummer developing business for every new spectacle; a publicity writer of freak incidents in the lives of stars and an expert on Paris gowns. He must record with great minuteness the number of new gowns worn. That these same new gowns are seen by the wives of the poor whose husbands do not earn in one year what one would cost, does not matter, for someday, you may wear a Paris creation if your husband becomes president or if the poorest miner's boy marries the president's daughter. And in the movies this happens daily; in fact, so engrossing is this make-believe-land to critics, pardon, movie reviewers, that they have long ago accepted it as the only existing world —and therein lies their futility, their sheer uselessness. They are absolutely unneeded today, except as publicity agents, in which respect they serve well. Here again, I wish to add that there are a few who have critical value. These are well known and respected.

And so, as the theatre critic serves his greatest purpose by indicating values to motion picture producers for popular consumption, the movie reviewer acts as the high pressure salesman to sell these effervescent commodities to the public under the guise of entertainment.

Throughout I have attempted to make clear that the social organization under which we live is responsible for the type of theatre, movie, and of critic developed. And because I find that it is impossible to segregate parts within a frame to show singular progress of any one thing, I am at this point uniting into one theme the theatre and the movies. They are both serving toward the same end, no matter what the approach may be.

Among the great powers of the world today there exist but two social states: Fascism and Communism. In Germany, Jugoslavia, Austria, Italy and Roumania, open fascist states; in all other capitalist countries fascist states hidden under more acceptable names. Recognizing no such thing as a social vacuity, countries are and must be today either communistic or fascistic. A neutral attitude cannot exist since there must be either progression or regression, and this sitting-on-the-fence, acting only as a deterrent to social progress, becomes automatically fascistic.

Germany and Russia nearest to each other and exemplifying advancing stages of Nazism and Communism are ideal for purposes of examination. In Germany the theatre before the advent of Nazism was for many years the most exciting in Europe. The experimental stage was the delight of artists from all parts of the world. New forms were continuously sought, spiral stages, advancing and retreating stages, three revolving platforms, modern settings. All this and more expressed the throbbing beat of a brilliant emotional and scientific origin. Today all this is ended. The remarkable decline in the vitality of the German theatre is one of the saddest and heart breaking sights to all who love the theatre, especially to all those who helped develop the theatre to the high level it occupied before Nazism.

But this may be shouted down with one word, generalities. To avoid this I offer factual information. State theatres in Germany were organized and supported by the state with a subsidy of fifty million marks and supported by the public in two major groups, the *Volksbühne,* numbering more than five hundred thousand members, a radical group, and the *Bühnenvolksbühne* comprising three hundred thousand members, the conservative group. There were also local audience groups supporting regional *Wanderbühne.* These organizations were the substance upon which the Nazi government attempted to build its National Socialist Theatre of propaganda. But this entire substance has now melted away so that there were evenings in the 1933–1934 season when the *Schauspielhaus* on the *Gendarmenmarkt* in Berlin, a theatre that spends three million marks a year of the taxpayers' money, had an audience of approximately one hundred. Box receipts which paid seventy per cent of the Berlin Opera's operating expenses dropped to thirty per cent in the same season.

Seriously concerned with this condition, the Nazi government attempted the bait of performances without cost. This was one of the great features of the "Power-through-Joy" institution. The people of Germany were interested in the critical cultural development that had been achieved by group organizations in the experimental theatre and which vanished of necessity when propaganda became the medium. The catch was that people would pay for enjoyment, but if bored would not attend free theatre.

First nights are dull. The anti-Nazi element now stay away and it was not the unthinking, believing Nazis who filled the theatres before, but the Communists, Liberals, Jews and Social Democrats. Even so, many would come, but in three years not one play of importance has been produced, not one playwright has appeared on the scene who could be classed as a dramatist of promise. And with the wonderful technique of past years to draw from, so stupid has every attempt been that the simplest of themes has ended in fiasco. The level reached was the jingoistic nonsense of *"Horst Wessel,"* a motion picture so bad that only the critics beneath the axe of the sartorially perfect executioner applauded.

What about the children's theatre? Surely countries that are so interested in protecting their newly discovered Aryan culture would be even more interested in enriching and securing this culture by establishing theatres for the young, training them, so that soon they might take their places, as the men and women so sadly needed to develop the now barren cultural forms. Instead the scene shows little men carrying large rifles trained for war. The culture of Germany has reached a climax, a devastatingly simple climax, that all brains can be wiped out by guns, making force more important.

This picture remains true with few changes for all imperialist countries; Germany is merely used as the outstanding example of rapid retrogression from its previous state. And more important is the fact that all imperialist countries will, of necessity, to protect a minority, follow in these footsteps. This must be prevented. Freedom of expression must be respected, and in this fight the theatre must be among the leaders.

In Japan today we find the same stifling influences at work. The Classical *Kabuki* drama is being favored above other and more recent forms. In these plays women are not permitted. It is entirely destitute of ideology or impli-

cations. It is an art of the past, featuring with its colorful
scenes, variety of musical accompaniment, female im-
personators and unique conventions; a form of drama
originating about 1600 and terminating before the dawn
of modern Japan, about 1868. The entire motif represents
and glorifies life during the feudal days. Realizing how
beneficial it must be to the militarists to keep the ancient
tommy-rot of hero-worship active, how does this in any
sense aid in the developing of a Nipponese drama appli-
cable to the scene of today?

In Soviet Russia the scene is different. A planned
theatre malleable to fit the shifting scenes of a hundred
different cultures was brought into being through endless
work. To clarify the scene thoroughly I shall take two
sections of Russia removed by thousands of miles from
each other, and indicate how planned theatres can flourish
in no matter what remote localities of the world they
may be in, one in Western Russia, the other in Central
Asia.

While in Berlin theatres stand empty, the Soviet Union
is planning two hundred theatres for the Ukraine alone.
In *Izvestia,* T. Medvedov, head of the culture and art
for the Soviet Socialistic Republic of the Ukraine, said,
"These future theatres according to the project will be
artistic creations in which all the cultural work of the
country districts will be centralized. The theatre build-
ings are planned so as to be adapted for the showing of
films, the production of plays and other spectacles, the
performance of concerts, the conducting of all cultural
and educational activities. A place is provided for the
orchestra, wash rooms for the artists, and even rooms

where guest artists will be able to stay overnight. There will be special quarters for mass work and libraries. The foyers of these theatres will be spacious, so as to eliminate all crowding and jostling. The best architects in the Ukraine have been chosen to execute this project. When the work of drawing plans for these theatres is completed the matter will come up for discussion before the meetings in all collective farms. None of these theatres is for the great cities of the Ukraine such as Odessa, Kiev or Kharkov, but for the villages of the collective farms."

Whether or not the scheme is carried out in full detail, these two hundred theatres are the most splendid testimony of the desire for culture newly awakened in the Russian masses and developed with them, for them, by the Communist organization.

In Central Asia, north of the Persian and Afghan borders, are the cities of Samarkand, Tokhara, Tashkent and Askhabad. Prior to the revolution there hardly existed any *Uzbek* theatre. What did exist was for the military and colonial families. Under the Czar all folk music was suppressed, every expression treated as that of a conquered people and regarded with disdain. Sheer stupidity for these people to feel that their art expressing their lives could in any sense parallel the charming, imported French farces! The censorship was very strict. Women were not permitted on the stage. *Dorvos,* rope walkers, flourished and theirs was the applauded art. Amateur groups made little headway and new mediums were not permitted.

After the revolution the entire scene changed. The flutes and the *barabans* still play in the tea houses but they also play in the modern theatre where their music has been woven, as has all other folk-art, into the pattern of new plays that picture the struggles, the triumphs of socialism in a world of ancient ways.

At the national Congress of Playwrights in Tashkent, problems relative to the *Uzbek* stage and its relation to the second five year plan were discussed. The ways and means of devising pageants and plays that would further the industrializing of the land and the pushing on to complete socialism were vital problems faced by young men and women interested in creating a theatre to meet the specific needs of the day. Every angle was thrashed out. Peasants were invited to state their views. Cross sections of the lives of the people were studied thoroughly, so that there would be no haphazardness in the presentations.

All theatres in Uzbek are under the Peoples' Commissariat of Education. All performers take an active part in the social tasks of the theatre plus the liquidation of illiteracy campaign. But the old forms are retained and where under the Czar, all folk music was suppressed, today there is a renaissance. The theatre, radio and motion pictures are all utilized to record this folk expression, and to campaign against illiteracy, provincialism and racial intolerance. To its varied nationalities, the modern playhouses in the distant corners of the union are of tremendous value in presenting problems in collectivism in terms of local culture. The leading companies travel throughout the country. Thus, in Moscow in one season can be seen the Gypsy, Turkish, Jewish, Georgian, Mongolian, Uzbek, Ukrainian, and other theatrical performances. Aside from its social themes this theatre embraces one of the most fascinating assemblies in the world. And now can be witnessed the first bloom of the freed centuries-old customs and habits that have formed the art background of these peoples.

At operas, at plays, at political meetings people are invariably intense, eager and stirred to emotion. They are never bored, because what they see is alive, it is filled with interests and ideas close to their hearts. The best entertainment is now available to them. Tickets do not go begging. Often a factory will buy out the whole house and the day before the director will come to the factory and discuss the aims and objectives of the plays so that the audiences will know what their comrades, the actors, are trying to accomplish. The same thing is true with operas. The libretto is explained and something of the music, and on the morrow, on velvet edge, sit workers; in one box sit punch-press operators, all women; in another welders, all men; and throughout the whole house there breathes the greatest of all achievements, unity toward knowledge.

The children's theatres are the psychological research departments for the future. Trained under the best present available methods they are carefully watched for responses. They select their own plays, by voting. Their comments, laughs, murmurs of disapproval are all tabulated and later reported. The ushers are children, as are the attendants. Every child has access to and is welcomed in these theatres.

There remains the theatres in Russian prisons, built by the prisoners themselves under the guidance of the

countries finest architects and builders. Of these a great
deal has been written, the excellence of performances,
the marvel of the backstage, the modernity of construction, all by men who heretofore had been regarded as
human waste. The reclamation of humans considered
worthless is a separate study, the parallel being strongly
visible in the progress made every passing day.

And now to return to the other countries. Everywhere
we witness the trying period in the theatre. Actors, playwrights, producers all live vicariously and productions
are sacrificed in nearly all cases for box office pleasure.
This in turn creates a worse bill of fare and results in
smaller audiences. But technically the theatre has halt-
ingly kept pace and offers many great possibilities for improvement. However, it needs financial support, and here,
it is, that the government represents the last hope for the
artist and theatre experimenter. It must have government backing, mass support to lift the drama from its
apathetic, pathetic position.

The situation witnessed was caused by competition
demanded of the theatre as it is of every parasitical form
of capitalism. There remained no place for the creators
of the drama except as exploitation value for promoters.
They owned the plays, the theatre, the real estate. They
were interested only in financial returns on investments.
Pyramiding, they eventually destroyed themselves and
forced their own emaciation of thought into the theatre. Revival must come from freedom, from mass expression, from government support.

The thought of movies, one of the largest industries,
under government supervision may sound slightly

prophetic. But, since they are a part of a present established frame, they must inevitably reach the same point as the theatre or any other unit, as for example, the giant railroads. This remains unarguable. Their birth and their ascendancy may be at present attributed to technical skill; for between an intelligent focus upon life as it actually exists and the hocus-pocus of the presentations, there has never been a reconciliation. Yet within this brief space of time, many of the major companies have been close to or in bankruptcy. The cry against the producer's extravagances is comparatively silly; these are not extravagances, but uncontrollable expenditures symptomatic of the entire system. Intelligence of purpose, knowledge of direction, control of resources cannot exist to any great extent. If they are present in individuals they are routed by the cumulative powers of today's system that makes it impossible for any individual to penetrate.

The movies upbringing has been rapid and they are now immersed securely, and passionately exploited. It follows, as the day the night, that they must collapse unless their present course is altered. This, however, is impossible. Novelties will not save them. Today they are as much of a public utility as electricity, and as such should be treated.

The movies should belong to the people and should mirror their lives. The movies should be one of the greatest weapons utilized for cultural and social advance. They must become international in their scope, in their portrayals of peoples and races. Profits must vanish from them. The arts, the technical brilliance, the high courage and purpose must remain. Realizing the present improbability of these hopes, I shall, like millions of others, wait for the inevitable social changes that will automatically forge the cinema into an entirely different influence than it exerts in the world today.

CHAPTER XV

THE MOVIES AND POLITICAL PROPAGANDA

by

UPTON SINCLAIR

I HAVE had dealings with the movies since their infancy. Twenty years ago the late Augustus Thomas made a really honest version of "The Jungle." That caused me to have hopes, but they were quickly dashed. I sold to a movie concern a story telling about a self-confident young rich man who made a wager that he could go out as a hobo and get a quick start in life. When I next heard of that story, it had to do with a lost will. Soon after the War, my old friend, Ben Hampton, historian of the industry, undertook to make a picture of "The Money-changers," which tells how the elder J. P. Morgan caused the panic of 1907. When I went to see it, it was a story of the drug traffic in Chinatown!

I don't think I am egotistical in saying that I have offered to the motion picture studios some good opportunities. "King Coal," "Jimmie Higgins," "100%," "They Call Me Carpenter," "Boston"—all these are motion picture scenarios ready made. There is only one thing wrong with them, they indict the profit system. "Oil" has been read by every concern in the business—I suppose a dozen agents have set out full of confidence to handle it, and never have they reported but one thing: "Magnificent, but dangerous."

That I know what I am talking about was proved when I happened to write on a subject that did not involve the profit system. Several concerns were bidding for "The Wet Parade" before the book was out. Metro-Goldwyn-Mayer paid twenty thousand dollars for it, and they spent half a million and made an excellent picture, following my story closely.

Now I loomed on the horizon, no longer a mere writer, but proposing to apply my rejected scenarios! While I was in New York some reporter asked: "What are you going to do with all the unemployed motion picture actors?" I answered: "Why should not the State of California rent one of the idle studios and let the unemployed actors make a few pictures of their own?" That word was flashed to Hollywood, and the war was on.

Louis B. Mayer, president of Metro-Goldwyn-Mayer, was vacationing in Europe when he got this dreadful news, and he dropped everything and came home to take charge of the campaign to "stop Sinclair." You see, he is chairman of the State Committee of the Republican party, so he had a double responsibility. I have met "Louie Bee," as he is called, now and then. I once took Bertrand Russell to lunch with him by invitation and learned that a great film magnate doesn't have time to talk with a mere philosopher, but politely appoints a substitute to see that he is properly fed and escorted round the lot.

Also Mr. Hearst was summoned from his vacation. Mr. Hearst belongs to the movie section. Hearst had been staying at Bad Nauheim. He was hobnobbing with Hanfstaengel, Nazi agent to the United States. You see, Hearst wants to know how the Reds are to be put down in America; so "Huffy," as they call him, flew with Hearst to interview Hitler.

As soon as Hearst learned of my nomination, he gave out an interview comparing me with the Pied Piper of Hamlin; and then he came back to New York and gave another interview, and from there to California, where he called me "an unbalanced and unscrupulous political speculator." His newspapers began a campaign of editorials and cartoons denouncing me as a Communist. I didn't see any denouncing me as a free-lover, and a menace to the purity and sanctity of the American home.

The first threat of the movie magnates was to move to Florida. Warner Brothers said they would go—and proceeded to start the construction of two or three new sound stages in Hollywood. Joseph Schenck of United Artists travelled to Florida to inspect locations, and the Florida legislature announced its intention to exempt motion picture studios from all taxes, and a mob of new "come-ons" rushed to buy lots.

Of course, this talk of moving was the veriest bunk. It would cost a billion dollars to move, and the British would grab the business meanwhile. Where would they get their mountains, and their eucalyptus trees, which represent the foliage of North and South America, Europe, Asia, Africa, and Australia? Above all, what would they do about the mosquitoes? I have lived in Florida, and I said to my audiences: "Right in the middle of a scene, one would bite the lady star on the nose and cost them fifty thousand dollars."

But that didn't keep them from building up the terror.

Orders for an assessment came; and in Hollywood an assessment means that the check is written for you, and you sign it. In this case it was for one day's pay of everybody in all the studios—except the big "execs." The total amount raised was close to half a million. There was a little rebellion, but I didn't hear about it in any paper in California. I had to go to the London *News-Chronicle* to learn that Jean Harlow and James Cagney were among the Protestants. From the same paper I learn that Katharine Hepburn was threatened with dismissal if she supported Upton Sinclair.

I am happy to say that a few Hollywood writers showed political independence. Frank Scully got up a committee in my support, and it was joined by Dorothy Parker, Morris Ryskind, Gene Fowler, Lewis Browne and Jim Tully.

Also they started in making newsreels. Will Hays sent a representative to attend to this. They invented a character called the "Inquiring Reporter." He was supposed to be travelling around California, interviewing people on the campaign. They were supposed to be real people, but of course they were actors. On November 4, the New York *Times* published a two-column story from their Hollywood press correspondent, from which I quote:

FILMS AND POLITICS

HOLLYWOOD MASSES THE FULL POWER OF HER RESOURCES TO FIGHT SINCLAIR

The City of Los Angeles has turned into a huge movie set where many newsreel pictures are made every day, depicting the feelings of the people against Mr. Sinclair. Equipment from one of the major studios, as well as some of its second-rate players, may be seen at various street intersections or out in the residential neighborhood, "shooting" the melodrama and unconscious comedy of the campaign. Their product can be seen in leading motion-picture houses in practically every city of the State.

In one of the "melodramas" recently filmed and shown here in Los Angeles, an interviewer approaches a demure old lady, sitting on her front porch and rocking away in her rocking chair.

"For whom are you voting, Mother?" asks the interviewer.

"I am voting for Governor Merriam," the old lady answers in a faltering voice.

"Why, Mother?"

"Because I want to have my little home. It is all I have left in the world."

In another recent newsreel there is shown a shaggy man with bristling Russian whiskers and a menacing look in his eye.

"For whom are you voting?" asked the interviewer.

"Vy, I am foting for Seenclair."

"Why are you voting for Mr. Sinclair?"

"Vell, his system vorked vell in Russia, vy can't it vork here?"

All these releases are presented as "newsreels."

Another "newsreel" has been made of Oscar Rankin, a colored prizefighter and preacher who is quite a favorite with his race in Los Angeles county. Asked why he was voting for Governor Merriam, he answered that he liked to preach and play the piano and he wants to keep a church to preach in and a piano to play.

Merriam supporters always are depicted as the more worthwhile element of the community, as popular favorites or as substantial business men. Sinclair supporters are invariably pictured as the riff-raff. Low paid "bit" players are said to take the leading roles in most of these "newsreels," particularly where dialogue is required. People conversant with movie personnel claim to have recognized in them certain aspirants to stardom.

At another studio an official called in his scenario writers to give them a bit of advice on how to vote. "After all," he is reputed to have told his writers, "what does Sinclair know about anything? He's just a writer."

Hitherto the movies have maintained that they could not do any kind of "educational" work; their audiences demanded entertainment, and they could have nothing to do with "propaganda." But now, you see, that pretense has been cast aside. They have made propaganda, and they have won a great victory with it, and are tremendously swelled up about it. You may be sure that never again will there be an election in California in which the great "Louie Bee" will not make his power felt; and just as you saw the story of "Thunder Over California" being imported from Minnesota, so will you see the "Inquiring Reporter" arriving in Minnesota, Mississippi, Washington, or wherever big business desires to ridicule the efforts of the disinherited to help themselves at the ballot-box.

Listen to the lords of the screen world vaunting themselves: The front page of the *Hollywood Reporter* eleven days prior to the election.

This campaign against Upton Sinclair has been and is dynamite.

When the picture business gets aroused, it becomes AROUSED, and, boy, how they can go to it. It is the most effective piece of political humdingery that has ever been effected, and this is said in full recognition of the antics of that master-machine that used to be Tammany. Politicians in every part of this land (and they are all vitally interested in the California election) are standing by in amazement as a result of the bombast that has been set off under the rocking chair of Mr. Sinclair.

Never before in the history of the picture business has the screen been used in direct support of a candidate. Maybe an isolated exhibitor here and there has run a slide or two, favoring a friend, but never has there been a concerted action on the part of all theatres in a community to defeat a nominee.

And this activity may reach much farther than the ultimate defeat of Mr. Sinclair. It will undoubtedly give the big wigs in Washington and politicians all over the country an idea of the real POWER that is in the hands of the picture industry. Maybe our business will be pampered a bit, instead of being pushed around as it has been since it became a big business.

Before Louis Mayer, Irving Thalberg, Charlie Pettijohn (a good old democrat under ordinary conditions) and Carey Wilson stepped into this political battle here, the whole Republican party seemed to have been sunk by the insane promises of Mr. Sinclair. With that group in the war, and it has been a WAR, things took a different turn. Governor Merriam's party here in the South had a HEAD, something that was missing before. It received the finances it so direly needed AND the whole picture business got behind the shove.

Sinclair is not defeated yet, but indications point to it, and California should stand up and sing hosannas for their greatest State industry, MOTION PICTURES, and that same industry should, for itself, point to its work whenever some of the screwy legislation comes up in the various State Legislatures during the next few months.

CHAPTER XVI

THE MOVIES AND THE COMMUNITY

by

JOHN HAYNES HOLMES

I

THE influence of the movies on the mind and morals of the community is so great as to be incalculable. This influence inheres, first of all, in the mere mechanism of the movies—the vividness of the impression which they make upon the observer! Of vast importance is the fact that the movies operate primarily and fundamentally through the organs of vision, the most potent of our physical senses. We remember not what we hear, nor even what we read, but primarily what we *see*. Then, too, in the case of the movies, there are the conditions surrounding the experience of seeing—conditions of such warmth and color and mystery and excitement, that the impression carried away is wellnigh indelible. It is not too much to say, from this point of view, that the movies constitute altogether the most powerful educational influence that exists in the modern world.

The influence of the movies is overwhelming, also, in its range as well as in its character. Thus, it is conservatively estimated that the moving picture theatres in this country have an audience of not less than thirty million men, women and children per week.* This means that one fourth * of the total population of the United States passes through the doors of the movie theatres, in city, town and village, every seven days. Compare this audience with the audience of a play which, if successful, may be seen perhaps by not more than five hundred thousand persons. An extraordinarily successful book, like "Main Street," or "Anthony Adverse," may sell several hundred thousand copies, and be read perhaps by over a million readers. There are popular magazines in this country, which have accumulated a total of more than two million subscribers and five million readers. Such figures as these, however, amazing as they are, do not come even within sight of the enormous number of people reached by the movies. Obviously, there is a problem of public influence here of greater magnitude than has ever before existed in the history of mankind.

The influence of the movies takes on a very especial significance when it is realized that the pictures make a peculiar appeal to children. Together with the radio and the newspaper comics, the movies are without question the chief influence which enters into the life of youth. The number of children who go to the legitimate theatres in New York, or in any other city, is relatively unimportant. The boys and girls who read adult magazines and books are comparatively few. But the youngsters who pour into our moving picture theatres are to be numbered by the millions every week. I am acquainted with such theatres, especially of the neighborhood or suburban

* According to latest estimates, the average weekly movie attendance in the United States is approximately seventy million.—Ed. Note.

variety, where at certain performances children are more numerous than adults. Certainly the proportion of children in adolescence who are in contact with the movies is unmatched by any other area in the field of **art.**

Both in character and in range of influence, therefore, in the life of the community, the movies present today a paralyzing phenomenon. That this phenomenon has been brought under our control is obviously not true. To a great extent it is still running wild, and overwhelming any counteracting influence along traditional lines of school, church, or society. At the moment it is more powerful than either the tabloid newspaper or the radio, and promises to remain so. For better or worse, we are today a movie-minded people. Business, politics, fashions, modes of conduct, standards of morality, types of thought, vice, crime, war and peace, all these and manifold other aspects of modern society are influenced today by the movies beyond any measure as yet made or even suggested. The destiny of our civilization may in the end hang upon the question of what this extraordinary industry may or may not do to us.

II

The influence of the movies upon the community is two-fold in the sense that it may be conscious or unconscious, designed or undesigned, direct or indirect.

The unconscious or indirect influence of the movies springs from the particular type of picture which may at any one time, in the regular course of trade, be coming from the movie studios. This type, whatever it may be, is largely determined by the intellectual and moral character of the writers, producers and directors of movie material. Seeking to provide entertainment, and incidentally to make money, the managers of this great enterprise, along with their innumerable associates and assistants, offer the public what, from the standpoint of their own character and experience as men, they think will make the widest and most successful popular appeal. They are undertaking to accomplish nothing but a firm basis for good business, and thus are directly serving no end but that of their own interests as profit-makers. All other interests are indirect and undesigned. It is in this sense that the movies exert what I have called an unconscious influence upon the public as determined by what the producers imagine the public want.

This unconscious or indirect influence of the movies has in many cases been excellent. From the early days of "Broken Blossoms," "The Golem," and "The Covered Wagon," to these later days of "Disraeli," "Cavalcade," "Little Women," and "David Copperfield," many fine pictures have appeared in our theatres. The producers and directors have in many cases done commendable and in some cases distinguished work. In the period of a single generation, this astonishing new industry has produced some great plays of its own and some great actors, which is as much as the legitimate theatre has done in any age. On more than one occasion, as I have watched the screen, I have seemed to catch anticipatory glimpses, so to speak, of a really great art which is destined to match the classic achievements of painting, poetry and music. Every now and then, that is, the door is opened upon a glorious landscape which is some day to be revealed to view.

But there came a time, some years ago, when this door became tight closed. The indecent era of the movies came along with the national era of prosperity. Hungry for money, the movie producers suddenly descended to levels of vulgarity and sheer obscenity, which did much to make the movie theatre a pornographic institution. The trouble was not so much the material actually used in the moving pictures during this period of indecency, for I doubt if there is any material in itself which is essentially indecent. I know of no phase of human life, in other words, however ugly or horrible, which cannot be used to high purposes and subdued to tragic, if awful, beauty. Nothing could seem to be worse than incest, and yet Shelley used this ghastly theme to noblest ends in his "The Cenci," the greatest poetic drama in the English tongue since Shakespeare. No, it was not so much the material used in the movies during this period which was bad, but the way in which this material, either good or bad, was used. Vulgar and dirty minds worked havoc everywhere.

Thus, the picture was smeared with filth. There seemed to be nothing too sacred, too beautiful, to be wantonly defiled by the gang of clowns and perverts who were in control at Hollywood. For years we had few pictures which did not, at some unfortunate moment, lift a curtain, so to speak, to show the leering countenance of the ignorant or salacious director behind the production. Murder was shown not as a tragedy, but as a legitimate occasion for excitement and revenge. Adultery was depicted not as a crime, but as an amusement for the rich, a game for the idle and luxurious, and a joke for everybody. Passion was presented not as poetry and romance and beauty, but simply as an incentive to lust and an excuse for the fleshy appetites of the body. And love, the noblest inspiration of music and poetry, the comfort and solace of the inmost hearts of men, was seldom revealed in its basic spiritual integrity, but almost invariably degraded to the level of mere animal sensationalism. I know of no experience quite comparable to that of seeing a movie theatre crowded with children screaming with delight as murder is justified, adultery adorned, and seduction taught. The cries in Dante's "Inferno" were not more terrible than these.

Also, the movies in this period, if not actually smeared with dirt, were prevailingly characterized by low manners, silly froth, and unspeakable distortion of reality. For years the pictures, even though not actually indecent, were debauched with overdoses, first, of sex, second, of crime, and third, of horror. Sex has its place in any normal and happy life, but life is not exclusively concerned with sex. Crime, unfortunately, is a conspicuous element of our contemporary civilization, but it does not as yet monopolize human interest. Horror now and again invades our homes and hearts, but it does not dwell there. I cannot take seriously an art which makes of the human story one uninterrupted round of seduction, fornication, adultery, racketeering, crime, and terror; and I tremble at the thought of the influence which such a presentation of the story must make upon the minds of those, adult and adolescent both, who are actually writing its unfolding chapters in the world of real experience.

It was the League of Decency, prudently conceived and ably organized, which ended this unhappy reign of debauchery in a great industry. Within a year after the League got to work, the movies were as if redeemed. The pictures were made clean of vulgarity and dirt, and presented some due sense of proportion and perspective in their presentation of the human scene. Best of all, great works of literature were suddenly found to be untapped mines of gorgeous entertainment, wholesome excitement, and noble imagination. The unconscious influence of the movies all at once became as good as it had been bad, and we came in sight, at least, of a new art to be added to music, painting, sculpture, and architecture as one of the regenerating influences of life.

III

But the influence of the movies may be conscious as well as unconscious, direct as well as indirect. Here is a great machine, in other words, which can be seized and deliberately manipulated to the accomplishment of certain definite ends designed and sought by those in control of its functioning. Influence of this kind may be best described in the one vivid and now terrible word, "propaganda." We learned the possibilities of propaganda during the Great War. We are just now beginning to learn its possibilities in time of peace.

What can be done with the movies in the propaganda spirit is being taught impressively by Soviet Russia. In that strange country the movies, like everything else for that matter, are in the hands of the government and are used almost exclusively for government purposes. Even the most innocent pictures have a hidden motive. Stories primarily conceived for purposes of entertainment are yet directed on the screen to the end of creating mind-patterns useful to the Bolshevist regime. The movies in Russia, in other words, are deliberately used as an educational influence for making a whole population of men, women, and children convinced Communists. There are to be no open minds in Russia, but exclusively minds molded to the design of Marxism. The value of the Marxian philosophy, its soundness or unsoundness, is not here in question. I am using it simply as an illustration of how the movies in one great country of the modern world have been captured by the government, and are being used, with malice or beneficence aforethought, to subject the people to one distinctive type of thought and life, to the exclusion of every other.

In America this use of the movies seems abhorrent, and Americans are inclined to rejoice that they are free from such subversive influences. But already it is becoming apparent that propaganda in the movies is not unknown in this country. Personal forces are at work which know exactly what they want to do, and are doing it triumphantly if not obtrusively. Take any current newsreel, for example! To what extent are the pictures in this reel free from the deliberate direction of those who are seeking to support the government, to advertise the army and navy, or to create some attitude favorable or unfavorable to ideas or trends of public policy? From 1933 on, the movies in America were practically surrendered to the Roosevelt administration, which was thus given full and free opportunity to use them to the uttermost to swing public opinion to the support of the New Deal. For years the movies have been at the disposal of the army and navy for the propagation of a favorable public attitude toward the abominable trade of war. It is not too much to say that it is impossible to see a newsreel, or release, in any theatre these days without seeing naval ships at target practice, bombing planes in active maneuvre formation, West Point cadets on parade, army units at home and abroad marching gayly down the street, and military or naval reviews with waving flags and martial music. It may be argued that these pictures are shown because they are thrilling and therefore have entertainment value. But it takes more than the innocence of little Eva to believe that such persistent exhibition of such military material as this is without direction and design. The movies are doing more to make war popular than any other single influence in our world today. And this influence is manipulated, as munitions are manufactured, by men who know exactly what they are doing and why. We have already learned that there will be no end of war, no durable conditions of peace, until the munition manufacturers have been put out of business. We have yet to learn that war will not be banished nor peace established until the movies have been rescued from the prostituting control of the military malefactors of our time.

I know of no more difficult problem than that of finding and marking the line between legitimate education on the one hand and subversive propaganda on the other. That the movies in their direct influence today are predominantly subversive propaganda, I am sure. That they can and should be used for legitimate educational purposes,

I am also sure. But I am not at all sure that the way has been found for accomplishing safely and surely this transition from the betrayal to the right guidance of the minds and lives of men. Of one thing, however, I am sure, and that is that the money-makers must be driven from the field. Commercialization is the real devil that is at work here. Until the movies are rescued from the hands of ignorant, coarse, vulgar, greedy men, who have no knowledge of literature, no understanding of human nature, no standards and ideals, and are in this business simply because they can use it for profit-making, and passed over into the hands of informed and high-minded men, who can make of this business a great art, it is certain we shall get nowhere.

IV

The modern community, unlike the ancient community, is not moved from within. On the contrary, to a paralyzing extent it is controlled from without. In the vast mechanisms of the printing press, the radio, and the movie, we see powers which have seized upon our society, and, like Frankensteins, are threatening to turn upon it and destroy it. The influence of these stupendous publicity machines, whether conscious or unconscious, direct or indirect, controls us instead of being controlled by us. I know of no greater or more necessary task than that of restoring our lives to self-mastery, that our communities may be free, and thus able to utilize to their own high ends of health and happiness these enormous powers which may be made so truly the servants of human destiny.

CHAPTER XVII

THE MOTION PICTURE AND SOCIAL CONTROL

by

SIDNEY E. GOLDSTEIN

THE PROBLEM

THE motion picture is not a sectarian but a social problem. The changes that have come during the last year in both the content and character of pictures have been due in large measure to the crusade of religious groups and mark one of the important victories of religious forces in America. Catholic, Protestant and Jewish organizations, however, are concerned and are engaged in common action not because the motion picture involves or violates religious doctrine; but because motion pictures today exercise a wide and profound influence upon the moral life of every community in the United States. The leaders of the Catholic Church, the Federal Council of Churches of Christ in America, and the Central Conference of American Rabbis all are of the same opinion, namely, that the motion picture is essentially a problem in social morality and must, therefore, be considered and solved in the field of social ethics.

The problem of the motion picture is not simple; on the contrary, it is exceedingly complicated, more so than most people believe. Each of the three divisions of the industry: production, distribution and exhibition of pictures is a large and difficult problem in itself. Some organizations are focusing their whole attention upon exhibition and the type of pictures each group in the community should see; other organizations are concentrating their efforts upon the weaknesses in the present system of distribution, especially upon block-booking and blind selling. To many of us, however, it seems wisest to start with production. We are convinced that if we can curb and control the evil at its source it will not be difficult to deal successfully with the questions of distribution and display. At the point of production the problem, when carefully studied, appears to be twofold: First, how can we prevent the production of pictures that are clearly a menace to the moral life of the community; second, how can we transform this miraculous invention of modern times into an instrument of clean entertainment, progressive education, and elevating art? If we can solve these two problems in the studio there will be fewer problems in the distributing center and in the local theatre.

LIBERTY

Some men and women believe that the solution of the motion picture problem lies in removing all restrictions and limitations. Let authors write what they wish; let directors produce what they please; and let corporations send forth and sell whatever they think will draw the greatest attendance and yield the highest profit. This is the plan that is proposed in the name of liberty. We who speak in the name of religion and social ethics also cherish dearly the principle of freedom and the liberties that are guaranteed to us under the Constitution: freedom of speech, freedom of the press, and freedom of assembly. We are convinced, however, that something more is involved in the problem of the motion picture than the principle of liberty. There is also involved the moral health of our children, the adolescents in our midst and the adults in the community. And we must remind the lovers of liberty that no man is free to spread disease in the city or in the country; this is the law of the Department of Health. Likewise no man should be free to maintain a source of moral contagion and to endanger the moral life and spiritual welfare of the people. Writers, directors and producers may resent this restriction upon their freedom; but they must recognize that there are many things men are not free to do even in the most liberal social state.

The fact is the law limits all our liberties in order to prevent them from degenerating into license. We are guaranteed freedom of speech, but we are not allowed to employ language that is libelous and damaging to the character of a man. We are guaranteed freedom of the press, but we are not permitted by law to print material, in word form or pictures, that is obscene. We are guaranteed freedom of assembly, but we may not come together to conspire against the Government. We are not free, in a Democracy, so to order our life or so to manage our property that our personal activities will jeopardize the welfare of the community. Law after law sets a limit upon our freedom of action in the interest of communal welfare or social progress. What the limit shall be the people themselves must decide from time to time through their law-makers and the Courts.

The Courts of New York State recently decided that there was no law making illegal the practices common in Nudist Clubs and Colonies. The Legislature immediately passed a Bill which outlawed these practices and thus set a limit upon the so-called liberties of men and women in the State of New York.

Men cannot be legislated into morality or made moral by law. This is the contention of those who advocate the end of all limitations and their contention is correct. But it is also true, and this the lovers of liberty must not forget, that men can be made immoral by exposing them to immorality, indecency, and obscenity. What the libertarians really demand is not liberty at all but the end of all law and limitation. They insist that they must be free to present the facts of life. They forget, however, that there are some facts of life that belong in the clinic, the dissecting-room and the pathological laboratory. Some men and women may find a morbid pleasure in studying the abnormal and the psychopathic; but this is no reason why they should feel free to portray these facts upon the public screen. It may be perfectly proper for a man to reveal the dark broodings of his spirit to a psychiatrist; but it is hardly decent for him to expose the distortions and perversions of his inward self to the public. Society has wisely constructed sewerage systems in order to save the surface of the earth from contamination and corruption.

Another thing to which we object in the libertarians is the treatment as well as the theme. The theme of the "Scarlet Letter" and "Othello" is the age-old theme of adultery; but both Hawthorne and Shakespeare treat these themes in such a way as to leave the reader or spectator purged and chastened. This is the method of all great artists. They take the acute problems of life and treat them in such a manner as to make the treatment a purifying and spiritual experience. The writers and directors and producers in Hollywood, on the other hand, take the same themes and treat them in such a fashion as a rule as to degrade themselves and to defile their audiences. They appeal to men and women upon the lower levels of life and send them forth in a lurid state of emotional tumult and mental confusion. They deal with the tragic problems of human relationships, but forget the statement of Aristotle that the purpose of tragedy is to purge the souls of men. What we expect from the artist is not a portrayal of the coarse and vulgar aspects of life, but an ethical interpretation of our common problems and our uncommon experiences. Either Hollywood lacks great artists or the artists are prostituting their powers to the wrong purposes.

CENSORSHIP

A second solution commended to the public is that of censorship. Here we must distinguish between official censorship by the Municipal, State or Federal Government, and the unofficial service rendered by volunteer groups or organizations. Up to very recently the screen carried before each picture the legend: "Passed by the National Board of Review." Nine out of ten men and women believed that the National Board of Review was an official body and that this body approved the picture presented. The National Board of Review, however, is not an organization authorized by Government; nor has it any official standing, nor does it, strange as it may seem, approve or disapprove the pictures that its members preview. It merely selects and classifies pictures as a service to its constituents. When we learned that this organization does not approve or disapprove any picture or any part of a picture we innocently asked the question: "What do you mean when you say 'Passed by the National Board of Review'?" The answer of the secretary was very direct: "It means we pass the picture on to the public." For previewing the films and passing the pictures to the public the National Board of Review, it is interesting to note, charges the motion picture corporations so much per reel.

This is but one example of the futility of such form of service. There are other groups, such as, The West and East Coast Preview Committees that are of equal value. These committees, composed of representatives of Women's Organizations on the Atlantic and Pacific Coasts, preview pictures and issue joint estimates of selected motion pictures for children, adults, and the family. These committees sitting in session from month to month and year to year must have seen the very pictures against which the country has protested and that resulted in the crusade of 1934. No word, however, ever came from them to caution the public. The truth is The West and East Preview Committees are too closely related to the industry itself to be of real value. While the members of the committees are drawn from the following seven organizations: The National Society of the Daughters of the American Revolution, The National Society of New England

Women, General Federation of Women's Clubs, California Congress of Parents and Teachers, Inc., The National Council of Jewish Women, The Women's University Club, Southern California Council of Federated Church Women, the committees themselves are in large part directed by representatives of the Motion Picture Producers and Distributors of America, Inc. These unofficial, unauthorized, and volunteer groups serve a purpose in selecting and classifying pictures. But they offer no protection to the public and mislead many men and women to believe that the community is properly safeguarded. If they protect and safeguard anyone, it is the Producer, Distributor, and Exhibitor, and not the public in whose interest it is assumed they act.

Government censorship is now operative in two cities: Boston and Chicago; and in seven States: Florida, Kansas, Maryland, New York, Ohio, Pennsylvania, Virginia. In some States, as in New York, the Board of Censors is a division of the Department of Education. Here, according to law, the Director is appointed by the Regents of the University of the State of New York upon the recommendation of the Commissioner of Education. There is no Federal censorship at present though from time to time Bills have been introduced into Congress that would create a Federal Board of Censorship for Motion Pictures; or that would place the motion picture industry under the control of a Federal Board similar to the Board that controls the railroads and the Commission that supervises the Radio. The code governing the motion picture industry under the N.R.A. does not deal with this problem except in Article VII which reads as follows:

ARTICLE VII—GENERAL TRADE POLICY PROVISIONS

Part 1. The industry pledges its combined strength to maintain right moral standards in the production of motion pictures as a form of entertainment. To that end the industry pledges itself to and shall adhere to the regulations promulgated by and within the industry to assure the attainment of such purpose.

Part 2. The industry pledges its combined strength to maintain the best standards of advertising and publicity procedure. To that end the industry pledges itself to and shall adhere to the regulations promulgated by and within the industry to assure the attainment of such purpose.

This does not constitute Government censorship; but there are a number of organizations in the United States that believe Federal Censorship is the one solution of the problem and that are persistently working from year to year for the passage of a Federal law that would establish Federal supervision and control.

In the cities and States in which censorship has functioned through a Government agency it has proved utterly ineffective. The records show that censorship bodies do reject some pictures in toto and compel eliminations in others. The latest report of the Motion Picture Division in New York, states that in the year ending June 30, 1934, 1769 films were reviewed. Of this number 15 were condemned outright and 286 were compelled to make eliminations before a license was granted. In spite of rejections and eliminations, however, it is evident that up to 1934 the censorship bodies passed picture after picture that aroused the wrath of the community and that eventually produced the nationwide protest and crusade. Through the years that the censors have been at work the country has been flooded with pictures that must be described as both vile and vicious, in spite of the fact that the law provides that no license shall be granted for a picture that may be classed in whole or in part as "obscene, indecent, immoral, inhuman, sacrilegious, or which is of such a character that its exhibition would tend to corrupt morals or incite to crime." Whether this is due to the composition of the Boards or to the standards the members employ is immaterial. The fact is that the experiments in governmental censorship have proved of no avail. In no way have they safeguarded children against pictures that incite to crime, that give to young men and women wrong standards of conduct, and that encourage even in older people incorrect conceptions of the problems of life. In view of this record, it is impossible to escape the conclusion that governmental censorship has failed.

Censorship through a Government agency, however, is not only ineffective; it is filled with dangers. It lends itself to a multitude of evils, only one of which is that it permits some one group to impose its own will upon the community. This is doubly dangerous when the group is composed of men and women who are under political control. It is one thing to protect ourselves against pictures that are indecent or obscene, or dangerous; it is altogether another thing to entrust to a man or a committee or a group the power to impose upon us their own standards of art and life. No group, whether it be selected by an official of the Government or by a Catholic, Protestant, or Jewish body, has the right to make mandatory upon the city or State or country standards that the group itself believes at the time to be correct. The Catholic Church, for example, strongly disapproves of pictures that deal with divorce and birth control and suicide, and is altogether right in urging its own communicants not to see pictures that deal with these themes. Other religious groups, however, do not regard these subjects in the same manner. Divorce, some of us believe, is the one way out of a degrading and humiliating marriage; and birth control, many of us are convinced, is a fundamental movement that has both social and scientific support. Censorship by the Government easily becomes an instrument of tyranny and cannot be tolerated in a Democracy. It creates more problems than it attempts to solve and must, therefore, be discarded as a solution of the motion picture problem.

SELF-REGULATION

The third solution of the motion picture problem is proposed by the industry, namely, self-regulation and self-discipline. In 1922, after repeated protests on the part of the people in different sections of the country, the larger motion picture corporations organized the Motion Picture Producers and Distributors of America, Inc. The purposes of this organization are described in the Certificate of Incorporation in the following paragraph:

"The object for which the Corporation is to be created is to foster the common interests of those engaged in the motion picture industry in the United States, by establishing and maintaining the highest possible moral and artistic standards in motion picture production, by developing the education as well as the entertainment value and the general usefulness of the motion picture, by diffusing accurate and reliable information with reference to the industry, by reforming abuses relative to the industry, by securing freedom from unjust or unlawful exactions, and by other lawful and proper means."

Mr. Will Hays was elected President and entrusted with the task of translating these purposes into motion picture practice. The public naturally assumed that Mr. Hays was given full power not only to build up the necessary staff of men and women but to establish a program of control that would protect the public.

There is only one way in which to test the work of this organization and that is by the events of the last thirteen years. During these years we have witnessed a constant repetition of the same cycle: protest, improvement, and lapse. Had each cycle resulted in a net-gain and some marked advance the story would not be so distressing. But the truth compels us to state that by 1934 the lapse in the motion picture industry had reached so low a stage and the pictures had become so utterly intolerable that the widest and most vigorous protest of all developed through the leadership of the Catholic Church and with the co-operation of the Protestant and Jewish groups. The staff of the Organization had passed picture after picture that ignored or violated every article in the Code of Production that the corporations adopted in 1930 and pledged themselves to observe. Some of these pictures, such as, the gangster series, were unpardonably dangerous; some of the pictures, such as, the sex series, were inexcusably filthy; others were just unbelievably stupid and contemptible. The least that can be said of the Motion Picture Producers and Distributors Organization is that up to the Spring of

1934 it had manifestly failed to achieve the purposes for which it was created.

The public rightly believed that Mr. Hays possessed power commensurate with his responsibility; but when the outburst came he pleaded that he lacked the authority to enforce his own decisions and to penalize the corporations that violated the Production Code. That he objected to the conduct of the corporations and tried to convince them that their program was both unwise and unsafe is no doubt true; but it is also true that in spite of all arguments and pledges corporation after corporation openly and audaciously violated every decent standard of life and contemptuously defied public sentiment. When Mr. Hays discovered year after year that he could not control the corporations included in the Motion Picture Producers and Distributors Organization he should at once have presented his case to the public. His primary obligation was not to the corporations that employed him but to the public that looked to him for protection.

Mr. Hays has now been granted additional power by the members of the Motion Picture Producers and Distributors Association and is in a position to impose a penalty of $25,000 upon any corporation that violates the decision of his organization. He has also reconstituted and greatly strengthened the committee of men that supervises the selection of topics and that approves the pictures. This committee, known as the Code Administration, of which Mr. Joseph Breen is Chairman, sits in Hollywood in daily session. These men review every subject and every scenario that is considered by the corporations and also passes upon every picture before it is released. In other words, the industry has subjected itself to a rigorous form of self-regulation and self-discipline. Mr. Breen and his associates appreciate the heavy responsibility that rests upon them and at the present time they are exercising a control that would have been regarded as incredible a year ago. Their decisions are definite and final and there is no appeal. If any pressure is exercised from the outside they resist it with courage and conscientiousness. There is no doubt whatever that the pictures now being released are free of coarseness and vulgarity, even if they are not scintillating with intelligence and vibrant with beauty.

The leaders of the motion picture industry also have come at last to understand the attitude of the American public. They realize now that the high attendance record and the large box-office receipt are not always an index of a picture's value or of the response of the whole community. The Mae West pictures were rated as successes and yielded a large return upon the investment. No pictures, however, did more to arouse indignation of the country as a whole. These pictures were temporarily and locally successful and profitable; but in the long run they have cost the motion picture industry ten times what the corporation gained in profit. This the leaders in the East and some of the leaders in the West are ready to admit and they are no doubt earnest and sincere in their desire to change the program of the motion picture industry and to establish new and higher artistic and ethical standards. Whether they fear the loss of their industry or have come to recognize the responsibility that rests upon men who control a vast and potent instrument of entertainment and education is not the question at present. The fact is that they are now convinced that unclean pictures are a danger to both themselves and to the community; and more than this, they have discovered, much to their surprise, that clean pictures artistically done, such as, "Cavalcade," "One Night of Love," and "David Copperfield," attract large audiences and yield more than a reasonable profit.

In spite of this change that has come about in both producers and the production-process we must frankly face the question: Is the improvement fundamental and permanent? Those of us who have been concerned with the problem during the last twenty years are not over-confident. In view of our experiences we naturally fear that the motion picture will again pass through the same cycle: protest, improvement and lapse to a lowel level. We realize, in the first place, that we are dealing not with a small group of leaders, but with a large company of men and women, in fact with the whole community of Hollywood, a community that is isolated from the rest of the country, that lives its own life, establishes its own standards, and is in constant danger of picturing not America but Hollywood upon the screen. In the second place, we are not satisfied that the change in the leaders in the East and some in the West means a change in the minds and hearts of the production managers, directors, and supervisors in the studios on the West coast and in the East. We who know the spirit of men are a little skeptical of the sudden conversions. In the third place, and this is the most important of all, we cannot forget that the members of the Code Administration are selected by, salaried by, and ultimately controlled by the corporations that compose the Motion Picture Producers and Distributors Organization. This central fact vitiates the entire system of self-regulation as a solution of the problem. We do not question the ability or the integrity of the men who compose the present Code Administration; but we do seriously question the system itself; and we cannot accept it as the much-needed and ultimate solution.

SOCIAL CONTROL

If unlimited license or Government censorship or self-regulation will not solve the motion picture problem is there some other solution? The beginning of the solution we believe lies in a recognition of the true status of the motion picture. The true status is found in the fact that the motion picture has ceased to be a private undertaking and has become a public enterprise. As a public enterprise the motion picture is invested, to use a legal term, with a public interest; but the public interest with which it is invested is far deeper than that implied in the law. At the beginning of 1935, according to the Film Daily Year Book, there were 13,386 motion picture theatres in operation in the United States. The average weekly attendance in these theatres totaled approximately 70,000,000. It is difficult to estimate how many different individuals this number includes, but it seems safe to assume that the motion picture must reach between 40,000,000 and 50,000,000 men, women and children every seven days. It enters into every city and town and hamlet and home, and exercises a deep and lasting influence upon the thoughts and feelings, the morals and the conduct of the great majority of the population. In view of the extent of its influence and the power of its appeal, to both the eye and the ear, the mind and especially the emotions of men, it must be counted as one of the mightiest forces in shaping and determining the conduct of the people. No other instrument or agency at our command is freighted with greater promise for good or omen for ill.

Most of us are accustomed to concern ourselves only with the child, with the danger to the boy or girl under sixteen; but we must not forget that adolescents and adults also come under the spell of the motion picture. Each group is probably affected in a different way and by a different type of picture. In general, it may be said that children escape the serious effects of the so-called sex pictures, but they are profoundly influenced by the gangster pictures. Children know more about gangsters and gunplay as a result of the motion picture than any child ought to know. The interest that is awakened in gangster movements and crime probably accounts in part for the large number of juvenile criminals that now compose the gangs in every city. The adolescents, on the other hand, are more deeply stirred by the sex pictures and pictures that portray Night Clubs, luxurious dens, and illicit escapades. One need only watch the adolescent group during the presentation of this type of picture to realize the reaction of youth and the degree to which their emotions are awakened and thrown into confusion by the picture material. Grown men and women, some may believe, are old enough to be immune; but not even adults can emancipate themselves altogether from pictures that deal lightly with the serious problems of life and that exploit wrong standards and perverted judgments. Ruskin once said that he became a lover of good pictures and a critic of art because his father never permitted him to stand in the presence of a bad picture. It ought to be clear that if men and women, young people and children, are constantly exposed to evil pictures they will not cultivate a love for what is good and clean and fine.

Because the motion picture is a public enterprise invested with a public interest the public must have a voice in shaping the policy that is to govern the industry and in turn influence the life of the people. One way in which the public is endeavoring to exercise social control is through The Better Films Council. The immediate objectives of this type of organization are well-expressed in the program of the Lower West Side Motion Picture Council in New York and of which Dr. Frederick M. Thrasher, Associate Professor of Education, New York University, is Chairman:

"1. To create interest in worthwhile motion pictures and in improving public taste both from the standpoint of more artistically adequate and less objectionable films.

2. To secure through a weekly Photoplay Guide the distribution to parents and teachers of advance information on pictures shown in local theatres indicating what films are worthy and desirable for adults, for family audience, for children.

3. The promotion of junior matinees and family week-end programs in accordance with principles already worked out in other communities and in co-operation with the Mayor in his attempt to work out a better plan with regard to the admission of minors under sixteen unchaperoned into motion picture theatres.

4. Wider use of films by churches and social agencies for educational purposes.

5. To help solve the particular film problems confronting local social agencies.

6. Wider use of motion pictures in visual instruction by schools and promotion of an interest on the part of schools in the development of motion picture appreciation through English or other classes.

7. Study and development of penny movies or a similar plan involving use of 16 mm. film, to keep children off the streets in order to reduce traffic hazards and to keep them occupied under supervision in a general program of crime prevention.

8. Development of an interest on the part of the local community in amateur movie-making as a wholesome and constructive hobby."

The Better Films Council program deals with the picture at the point of display; and undoubtedly will build up sentiment in support of good pictures. This in turn may lead to a protest against bad pictures, but the program itself is too new for us to be able to test its effect upon the industry.

The boycott is another method of social control that has been employed in limited areas and by limited groups. There is no doubt whatever that the boycott can be developed into a powerful weapon against local theatres and even against a group of theatres in a local community. It means a loss of patronage, and the loss of patronage means an immediate loss of profits. No motion picture theatre or group could long stand out against this form of social attack. The chief difficulty with the boycott is that it requires a highly organized and thoroughly disciplined group for its enforcement. The Catholic Church in Philadelphia was undoubtedly able to employ and to enforce the boycott because of the excellent organization of the Catholic Church and the splendid discipline of its members enrolled in the Legion of Decency. Neither the Protestant nor the Jewish groups possess a similar organization or discipline and, therefore, could not hope to achieve a similar result. The Federal Council of Churches through its Committee on Motion Pictures prepared a Declaration of Purpose to be distributed to members of the Protestant churches which reads as follows:

"I wish to join with other Protestants, co-operating with Catholics and Jews, in condemning vile and unwholesome motion pictures. I unite with all who protest against them as a grave menace to youth, to home life, to country, and to religion.

I condemn absolutely those salacious motion pictures which, with other degrading agencies, are corrupting public morals and promoting a sex mania in our land.

I shall do all that I can to arouse public opinion against the portrayal of vice as a normal condition of affairs, and against depicting criminals of any class as heroes and heroines, presenting their filthy philosophy of life as something acceptable to decent men and women.

I unite with all who condemn the display of suggestive advertisements on bill-boards, at theatre entrances and the favorable notices given to immoral motion pictures.

Considering these evils, I declare my purpose to remain away from all motion pictures which offend decency and Christian morality. I will try to induce others to do the same.

I make this protest in a spirit of self-respect, and with the conviction that the American public does not demand filthy pictures but clean entertainment and educational features.

That there may be a united front, the pledge of the Legion of Decency has been used with only slight changes. Organizations and individuals are free to formulate their own pledges. The important thing is not the form of a pledge but to keep its purpose."

The change that has come about in the motion pictures, however, within the last year has made the employment of this program unnecessary. That a small community can be organized and moved to boycott the motion picture is reasonable to expect. The more homogeneous the community, the more reasonable is the expectation. But that the boycott can become an effective weapon in a large community composed of different racial, religious, national and social groups is exceedingly doubtful unless the motion picture sinks to a much lower level than it did in the Spring of 1934.

A third method through which the public is endeavoring to exercise control is legislation governing the distribution of motion pictures. This legislation deals largely with the trade practice of block-booking and blind selling. This program has been urged chiefly by the Motion Picture Research Council and is best expressed in a Bill introduced into the House of Representatives by Mr. Pettengill March 6, 1935.

"To prohibit and to prevent the trade practices known as 'compulsory block-booking' and 'blind selling' in the leasing of motion-picture films in interstate and foreign commerce.

Be it enacted by the Senate and House of Representatives of the United States of America in Congress assembled.

That the methods of distribution of motion-picture films in commerce whereby (*a*) exhibitors are required to lease all or a specified number of an offered group of films in order to obtain any individual desired film or films in the group, a trade practice sometimes known as 'compulsory block-booking,' and (*b*) films are leased before they are produced and without opportunity for the exhibitor to ascertain the content of such films, a trade practice sometimes known as 'blind selling,' are hereby declared to be contrary to public policy in that such practices interfere wth the free and informed selection of films on the part of exhibitors and to prevent the people of the several States and the local communities thereof from influencing such selections in the best interests of the public, and tend to create a monoply in the production, distribution, and exhibition of films. The Congress finds and declares that such methods and practices adversely affect and constitute a burden upon commerce, and it is the purpose of this Act to prohibit and to prevent such methods and practices in commerce."

If this Bill were to pass, and it is most unlikely, it would end one of the greatest evils in the motion picture field. In spite of all protests to the contrary on the part of motion picture corporations and the Hays organizations, motion picture exhibitors are compelled by contract to rent pictures in large blocks and to rent them not only without seeing the pictures, but long before the pictures themselves are produced. This not only places the exhibitor at the mercy of the producer but makes it practically impossible for a community to secure the pictures that it desires to see and has a right to demand. The clause in the Code that permits a return of ten per cent of pictures is so restricted as to render it in practice null and void. This is the judgment of the exhibitors who have attempted to exercise the right of cancellation.

The Better Films Council working at the exhibition stage and legislation designed to end evils at the point of distribution are not in themselves sufficient to solve the problem of the motion picture. In order to complete the program of social control it is necessary to create an agency that will deal with the problem at its source, that is, at the center of production. For this purpose we propose a committee that will have the authority to supervise the selection of themes and the approval of pictures in the name of the public. This committee should be composed of representatives of the industry, education and the ministry and should consist of men and women who are liberal-minded students of social psychology and social ethics. It is always dangerous to name individuals but it ought not to be dangerous to suggest that the men and women to constitute this committee should be of the type of Dr. Richard Cabot, of Harvard University, Professor Harry Overstreet, of City College, New York, Dr. John Dewey, Dr. John Haynes Holmes, of the Community Church, Rabbi Stephen S. Wise, of the Free Synagogue, and Archbishop McNicholas, of Cincinnati. In order that the committee may in no way be subject to the subtle, insistent and well-nigh, irresistible pressure generated by the industry, the men and women must not be selected by the Corporations nor salaried by the Corporations nor in any way directly or indirectly controlled by the Corporations. This Committee on Supervision of Production is sufficiently important from the point of view of public policy to be selected and appointed by a group of men and women composed of the Presidents of the leading Universities in America. Its primary responsibility will be not to the industry but to the public, and its chief concern will be not with what the Corporations want but with what the public needs.

This public Committee on Supervision should be empowered to do two things: First, to revise and reformulate the Code of Production. The present Code that governs production was adopted in 1930 and must be described as little more than a crude and amateurish attempt to establish standards. A committee of experts in the field of social psychology and social ethics, fully aware of the dangers that threaten the great mass of people through misused agencies of appeal and propaganda, could be trusted to agree upon a set of general principles and to develop a code of guidance that would reflect the moral judgment of the great majority of the people in America. These men and women would not always agree upon the topics that should be included within the province of motion picture production; but they would undoubtedly co-operate with each other in excluding from the screen all material that normal people recognize as vulgar and vile and vicious and a danger not only to the individual but also to the family and to group relationships. They would understand that the motion picture has become something more than a means of entertainment and recreation; that it is essentially an instrument of education and of art, and even more than the press and the radio operates as a penetrating and pervasive force throughout social life. They would construct a Code that would not permit the motion picture to be prostituted to the making of profits or employed to advance the special interests of groups that are in control of our economic life.

The Code of Production, however, no matter how well conceived and constructed, would be of no avail unless it were enforced by a staff of men and women who were thoroughly in sympathy with its principles and its spirit. This is the second thing that the Committee on Supervision should be empowered to do: to appoint and supervise the Executive Staff that is to enforce the Code. This staff must be built up of men and women who are carefully trained, widely experienced and altogether competent. The criticism of scenarios and the approval of pictures cannot be left to members of volunteer organizations or to untrained, inexperienced and incompetent scribes and clerks. We are here concerned with the moral life and the spiritual welfare of nearly half the population directly and the whole of the population indirectly. This tremendous and impressive fact should lead us to demand the highest type of service that can be secured, no matter what the cost to the community. The community and the country does not count the cost of protection against disease and epidemics; the prevention of disease and the promotion of health have now become so important in community life that we establish schools in which to train men and women for expert and responsible service in the health field. It would not be difficult for the Departments of Social Science, Psychology and Ethics in our leading Universities to train men and women for the form of service that should be expected of members of the Executive Staff. If one tenth of the extravagant salaries that are now paid to actors and executives were spent in preparing men and women to properly criticize and appraise motion pictures, the community and the country would be adequately safeguarded against moral contagion and ethical disintegration.

Conclusion

The conclusion to which we come, after surveying the different solutions offered us, is that unlimited license, Government censorship, and self-regulation on the part of the industry have all proved ineffective and are doomed to fail. They cannot protect the public against the dangers of evil pictures; nor are they able to lift the motion picture to the level of clean entertainment, progressive education and inspiring art. The point at which to begin a program of reconstruction, it is now clear, is not exhibition or distribution but production; and production must be brought under social control, under control, that is, of a group of men and women who will supervise the production of pictures solely in the interest of community welfare and social progress. The Motion Picture Corporations, we are well aware, are not at present in the mood to accept this solution of the problem; they still insist upon the right of self-regulation through the Hays organization. They do not seem to understand that through their repeated failures and offenses during the last twenty years they have forfeited the right to regulate an industry and to fashion the policy that is to govern a great public enterprise. The time is very near at hand when they will be compelled to face the choice of social control on the one hand or Government censorship on the other. In order to escape Government censorship we trust that they will choose social control. If they do not make the choice themselves, it is not unlikely that the choice will be made for them.

The present protest against the motion picture, men must understand, is unlike other protests in the past. It is not a sporadic and isolated outburst of public sentiment against a single evil; it is nothing less than one phase of a great wave of moral wrath that is sweeping wide and deep through every segment of life. Everywhere people are protesting against incompetency and corruption in our political system; they are protesting against oppression, exploitation and injustice in our economic organization; and they are also protesting against debasement and degradation in our cultural agencies and institutions. These protests are not surface symptoms; they presage a new awakening and resurgence in our ethical life and a veritable Renaissance of the spirit. The people are determined to assume control of their political, economic and cultural life; they are determined to socialize all the instruments and processes of society as they have already socialized education; and most of all they mean to employ these instrumentalities in the maintenance of democratic programs and in the advancement of democracy. The motion picture, together with the radio and the press, under social control, will be transformed into servants of the new social order that is emerging out of the confusion into which the old and outgrown system has finally collapsed.

CHAPTER XVIII

WHAT DO THE CHILDREN THINK
OF THE MOVIES?

by

W. E. BLATZ

WHEN Mark Twain passed his casual remark about the
weather "Everybody talks about it, but nobody seems to
do anything about it," he was wittier than he was accurate.
Before his day and especially since, man has done a great
deal about the weather, roofs keep out the rain and snow,
refrigerators and fans keep our homes, theatres, trains and
food cool in summer, furnaces heat them in the winter,
we build summer resorts beside cooling bodies of water,
we reforest to preserve moisture, we explode the ice in
the St. Lawrence, and try to explode the clouds to bring
rain and in lieu of direct control we insure ourselves
against rain, hail, tornadoes or sunshine. This has not prevented us from talking about the weather which is perhaps the worst feature and the most difficult to eradicate.

And so with the movies. At present they are with us
as inevitably as the weather and everybody talks not only
about them but invariably against them. The harm they
do, the evil they promulgate, the degrading influence they
manifest and the unutterable passions and crimes that they
arouse and instigate. The question is, "What are we
going to do about it?"

We can no more eliminate the movies than we can the

weather. But just as we can enjoy and benefit by the sun, the rain, the snow and the winds, so we can enjoy and benefit by the movies whether fair or foul.

But before we enter into the controversy it seems that we should know more about the movies as they affect the audiences. The most serious criticism is directed towards the effect of the movies upon children and we will confine our interest and remarks to this phase of the problem in this chapter.

In the first place it seems in order to ask how much of the time at the disposal of children is spent attending movies. This is a legitimate question because the movies are only one influence and may be expected to affect the devotee more or less directly as the time spent in this activity. Just as the home wields an influence, and the school and the church and the Y.M.C.A. Other things being equal one might expect the influence which acts over the longest period of time to affect the organism most readily and permanently.

The data, from a survey of over 2000 school children between the ages of 9 years and 19 years for a period of three months during the winter of 1934–35 in Toronto, is presented in the form of a graph.[1]

Examination of this graph shows that 9-year-old children attend the movies 1.5 times in 3 months. There is a gradual increase in the frequency of attendance to the age of 15. The children of this age attend 9.4 times in three months, or a little oftener than once a week. From

---

[1] The details concerning the connection of this data are reserved for a more technical paper. All of the material was anonymously obtained so that the approval or disapproval of adults were equally avoided.

The Movies on Trial

this peak there is a gradual decrease in frequency with age. In Table I the same results are tabulated in such a

GRAPH I.

FREQUENCY OF MOVIE ATTENDANCE PER 3 MONTH PERIOD

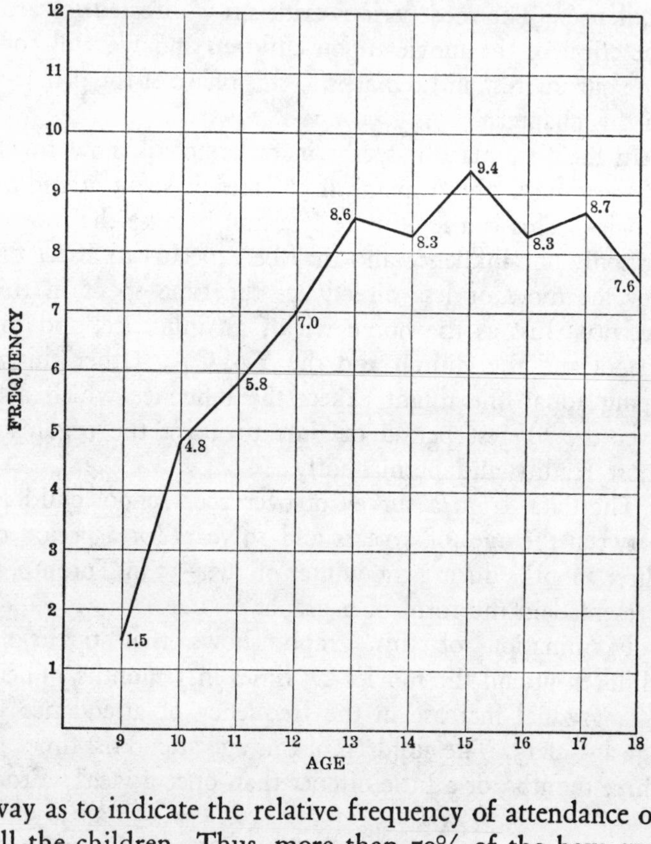

way as to indicate the relative frequency of attendance of all the children. Thus, more than 50% of the boys and more than 60% of the girls do not attend the movies oftener than once in 2 weeks in the winter time. And only 7% of boys and 3% of girls attend oftener than once a week.

Now, it cannot surely be intimated that the relatively short time that children spend in the movies, even if their influence were wholly bad, could counteract the good in-

TABLE I.

PER CENT FREQUENCY OF MOVIE ATTENDANCE

	2 OR 3 TIMES WEEKLY	ONCE WEEKLY	ONCE IN 2 WEEKS	ONCE A MONTH	ONCE IN 3 MONTHS	NEVER
Boys . .	7	41	27	13	8	4
Girls . .	3	36	28	18	9	6

fluence of home, school and church. And if it is asserted that this short time is concentrated propaganda, then the home and school and church authorities should attend oftener and discover just what technique is employed to accomplish this result. Then they could use it to advantage in their own milieu. We should like to contend that children go to the movies to be entertained, just as adults do, and that the contention that they attend to store up all the evil they can discern for the purpose of perpetrating it upon an unsuspecting and innocent community is gross nonsense. We will have more to say about this later.

Table II shows some rather interesting trends in the companionship of movie-attendance. The younger children, especially the girls, attend the movies with their parents most often. There is a gradual emancipation with age which is perhaps a healthy sign. The fifteen year old boys attend alone in 22% of cases. The girls seldom attend alone especially as they grow older. We can only conclude that this table shows that on the whole the parents are sufficiently interested in this activity of their children to supervise it adequately and yet not to enclose

TABLE II.

COMPANIONSHIP

AGES	9-10-11	12-13	14-15	16-17	18-19-20
Boys					
with Parents .	32%	16%	21%	12%	9%
with Comp. .	59%	73%	57%	80%	77%
Alone .	9%	11%	22%	8%	14%
Girls					
with Parents .	64%	34%	26%	16%	0%
with Comp. .	35%	63%	69%	84%	100%
Alone .	1%	3%	5%	0%	0%

the child in a parental censorship which would not only destroy some of the entertainment-value but would prevent the development of individual evaluation and good judgment.

As evidence that this judgment is developing and that these children have perhaps as keen if not a keener sense of entertainment and good taste as could be desired the following plan was adopted. The children were asked to rate the various types of movies according to their desirability. In other words, "Which type of movie would you like to see at your neighborhood theatre."

The three most preferred in 1, 2, 3 order and the three least preferred in 9, 10, 11 order are shown in Tables III

A and B. It will be seen that comedy is the first choice of children up to the age of thirteen years, then mystery

TABLE III. A

LEAST PREFERRED

	9TH	10TH	11TH
10	Gangster	Love Interest	Classical
11	Gangster	Spectacle	Love Interest
12	Gangster	Spectacle	Love Interest
13	Classical	Love Interest	Spectacle
14	Gangster	Love Interest	Spectacle
15	Classical	Spectacle	Wild West
16	Love Interest	Wild West	Gangster
17	Love Interest	Gangster	Wild West
18	Gangster	Spectacle	Wild West
19	Gangster	Spectacle	Wild West

TABLE III. B

TOP PREFERENCE

	1ST	2ND	3RD
10	Comedy	Musical Comedy	Mystery
11	Comedy	Historical	Mystery
12	Comedy	Mystery	Musical Comedy
13	Comedy	Mystery	Musical Comedy
14	Mystery	Comedy	Musical Comedy
15	Musical Comedy	Mystery	Comedy
16	Comedy	Musical Comedy	Historical
17	Musical Comedy	Mystery	Comedy
18	Musical Comedy	Comedy	Historical
19	Musical Comedy	Mystery	Historical

movies and then musical comedy. Musical comedy usurps first place for the older children. It is interesting and illuminating to study the least preferred types, especially the inclusion of gangster and love interest movies in the younger children. Also, love interest is 11th at age of 11 and 12 years, 10th at age of 13 and 14, and 9th at age 16 and 17, and has moved into a more preferred category from 18 to 19 years but does not reach the most preferred class at any age.

It can only be concluded from these data that the children are forming their own judgments and do not see in the movies all of the implications of the adult mind, or if they are perceived, they receive the notice that we, as adults, hope they deserve. We may criticize the comedies as of a low order of intelligence or the musical comedies as brazen, jazzy and cacaphonous but these children are maturing and will pass through this phase of entertainment awaiting more mature offerings from a sophisticated and cultured adult world.

It is evident that these children are not seeking the crime and sordidness and spectacles of human frailties but are looking for brightness, laughter and song, and dance. They are interested apparently in the macabre and mysterious, but who is not? They are certainly stimulated in this interest by the daily newspaper, which offends in this respect, as well as in good taste, far more than any movie. Perhaps we should congratulate ourselves that this aspect of life is still news in the daily press and still novel as movie material.

In order to verify the results of the above preferences the children were asked to check a list of 16 movies which had been presented in Toronto during the period of the study. They were further requested to indicate whether they enjoyed the presentation and if not to write briefly what part was offensive or displeasing. Table IV shows

8 of these movies arranged in order of preference for both boys and girls.

It will be seen that "The Count of Monte Cristo" was the universal favorite; that "One Night of Love" was most frequently attended; also that the children showed some

TABLE IV.

JUDGMENT OF MOVIES AFTER VIEWING

MOVIE	GIRLS		BOYS		TOTAL		PER CENT DISAPPROVAL
	number		number		number		
	who saw movie	who did not enjoy	who saw movie	who did not enjoy	who saw movie	who did not enjoy	
Count of Monte Cristo	176	1	329	3	505	4	.8%
Gay Divorcee . . .	190	12	267	16	457	28	6.6%
Ann of Green Gables .	227	3	124	21	351	24	6.8%
One Night of Love . .	288	9	333	45	621	54	8.7%
Chu Chin Chow . .	158	27	267	29	425	56	13.1%
Chained	104	22	96	24	200	46	23.0%
I'm No Angel . . .	132	38	282	62	414	100	24.1%
Crime Without Passion	31	10	92	31	133	41	30.8%

discrimination in their choice of pleasing entertainment; "Crime without Passion" attended least frequently of all and with 30% disapproving. Mae West, however popular with adults, does not seem to have the same appeal to the youth of the country. The boys were not as favorably impressed with "Ann of Green Gables" as the girls. This is also true of Grace Moore.

One cannot be terribly perturbed when the youth of the city prefer a masterpiece like the "Count" and the musical excellence of "One Night of Love" to the others lower on the list.

But a far more significant group of data was forth-coming. The children were asked to choose between going to the movies and participating in 16 other activities, as shown. The results of this voting or choosing are illuminating as shown in Table V.

TABLE V.

LIST OF ACTIVITIES EVALUATED IN TERMS OF "THE MOVIES."

A. *Preferred by the boys and girls of all ages 9–19 years:*—
   1. Attending the Canadian National Exhibition.
   2. Riding horseback.
   3. Skiing.
   4. Attend a hockey match.
   5. Swimming.
   6. Skating.

B. *Preferred by boys, but not by girls:*—
   1. Play football.
   2. Play hockey.
   3. Fishing—(including girls up to 12 years).
   4. Attending football match—(including girls about 14 years).

C. *Preferred by girls, but not by boys:*—
   1. Attending a picnic—(including boys up to 13 years).
   2. Dancing—(including boys over 15 years).

D. *Both boys and girls prefer attending movies to:*—
   1. Attending Symphony Concert—(except girls over 18 years).
   2. Listening to radio.
   3. Going for auto-ride—(except girls and boys under 12 years).
   4. Reading a good book—(except girls up to 16 years).

Thus all of the children from 9–19 voted overwhelmingly at all ages in favor of the activities in Group A.

All of the boys would rather participate in Group B activities than attend movies; as is true of the girls with reference to Group C. The vote was overwhelmingly in favor of movies compared to a symphony concert, the radio, car riding and reading with the exceptions noted.

The conclusion to be drawn from this table is obvious. The movies are second best choice in 12 of 16 activities. In a community or in a home where these activities are provided and fostered the movie becomes an adjunct to the entertainment needs of the child and never the primary factor. Where these activities are not available the child of necessity chooses the movies as the next best outlet and should not be blamed for his choice. The "movie-habit," *i.e.,* going to the movie every Friday night no matter what picture is being presented, will be found in homes and communities where there is a dearth of other opportunities for relaxation, leisure and entertainment. This "habit" is a sign of imaginative sterility and should be pitied rather than condemned. It is also rather interesting to find in a community as supposedly cultured as is Toronto to see that the children prefer the movies to Symphony concerts and to constructive reading. Surely the children have arrived at these choices through imitation and training.

Now these are the facts as we have them placed before us. To sum up, young children and adolescents do not attend the movies any more frequently than the legitimate demands of entertainment permit. Where the frequency of attendance is high it usually indicates a dearth of other activity opportunities; the supervision by parents in the younger years is sufficient to preserve a family unity of cultural standards and yet provides adequately for a healthy latitude in individual tastes; the choice of movies by children shows satisfying and discriminating attitude when the comedies (including the Silly Symphonies, Mickey Mouse and other Walt Disney offerings) and singing and dancing show such an appeal; and lastly when the movies as entertainment-value still fall below other participating activities as skating, dancing, hockey etc. there is little to fear in the developmental trend of the coming generation.

The question now arises, does a child who attends the movies derive from this source a mental content which leads to vice, crime or delinquency? There is no doubt that the phenomenon of identification occurs during the viewing of a movie-show as with all other experiences. Just as the boy imagines himself as Lindbergh, or Babe Ruth, or Tilden, or Byrd, he imagines himself the gangster leader, the lone wolf, the oriental demon, or Frankenstein, and the girls become Wills, Marie of Roumania, Putnam, or Madame de Maintenon, the gangsters' Moll, or one of the wives of Henry VIII. But identification during a short period of flight-from-every-day-life does not mean assuming the role permanently *in* every-day life. Reality is too overpowering for this to occur. We seldom share our thoughts for fear of ridicule, much less manifest them in activity and thus expose ourselves to the gibes and satire of our friends or enemies.

Undoubtedly, as Thurstone and others have shown, a movie may for a time alter the attitude of the spectator towards some aspect of life, *e.g.,* race prejudice, but so also do politicians, ministers, newspapers and parents. The amazing aspect of this effect is its impermanence and evanescence.

In eight years' close association with the Juvenile Court Clinic in Toronto, we have on no occasion been able to lay the specific act of delinquency at the door of the movie theatre. After all, the pictures do not show how to open a school locker, to swipe a quarter, or illustrate how to break open a paper box, or how to take apart a stolen bicycle, or shy coal at the brakeman, or trespass. If movies did descend to these behavior categories the children would not attend. They want romance, adventure, incredibilities, impossibilities not so that they can imitate but so that they may vicariously enjoy what they have no hope of living.

No one would encourage movies which are in bad taste. Whether they so offend or not depends upon the cultural level of the community. But after all, nothing could be more indicative of the general low level of public taste than the rather disgusting advertisements that repeat themselves literally *ad nauseum* in our magazines—advertisements that refer to bodily odors, gastric, and lower functions, disembowelled X-ray photographs and so-called hygiene of an intimate character. Personally, we have never seen a movie scene depict any of these phenomena. Furthermore the movie is not, thank goodness, an uplift device. It is for entertainment. If a "higher" level of activity is desirable, and perhaps this is a debatable point, then the energy must be expended by those agencies whose function it is to initiate and execute such movements.

But—the proper method is not to attack other agencies.

The home, the church, the school, the university, the Club, all have an influence on the general level of aesthetic appreciation and cultural appetites of their constituents. Prohibition has never been a means of training. Human beings will respond positively and avidly to *any* situation which provides change, novelty and an opportunity for satisfying curiosity and experiment. The agencies or institutions mentioned above can so arrange the milieu for children that they will be so busy doing many things that the lure of passive entertainment will be confined to things worthwhile. The movie then will have to compete with these other activities and will survive on its merits. Censorship, prohibition and boycotting have always assisted the unworthy to survive. When the industry can produce a masterpiece like "The Bengal Lancers," why should it fear any sort of criticism? That all releases are not masterpieces is self-evident and self-explanatory. Homer sometimes nodded. But just as it is absurd to stand in wonder at *all* early Italian art or decry *all* modern neo-realism so it is rather infantile to expect *all* movies to be excellent or to condemn them *all* because someone's judgment was at fault in delivering another which might better have been left in utero. After all, attendance at movies is not yet compulsory.

It is not within our scope or capacity to suggest to the movie industry what should be done about the movies. Too many people, and usually the wrong ones, have attempted this with indifferent success. A novelist writes a book, tries to find a publisher, who tries to find a market. The legitimate stage succeeds or fails on the merits of the production, the cast and the playwright; an invention works and sells itself or not. Why the movie industry imagines the general, unskilled public should do anything beyond attending the theatres or staying away from them is a curious phenomenon.

We do not consider the movies a menace to children or adults. In any community in which this attitude is patently manifest, this article points the way to a solution of the problem, *viz.* make the leisure time of the child so complete and interesting that sitting down and watching some one else enjoy the celluloid adventures will pale into ghostly insignificance as compared to real life. This is a difficult and perhaps a futile ideal because after all, we are none of us so fertile in imagination and phantasy that we cannot learn and thrill to another's genius in this respect. Until some one devises a more pleasing, a more efficient and more thrilling technique for passing on these delights, than the movies, they will remain with us and will influence us for good or ill depending largely on how we have been trained to interpret them.

CHAPTER XIX

HOLLYWOOD CLEANS HOUSE

by

CHAPIN HALL

MORE people are interested in the motion picture industry than in any other one enterprise in all the world.

Not in the mechanical or artistic details of production, although that phase has a tremendous following, but in the pictures themselves and the actors who bring them to life.

In twenty years they have remodeled civilization's concept of entertainment, have brought a make-believe world to the door of practically every citizen of the world.

In this country one-fifth of the population go to the pictures at least once each week.[1]

Here in Los Angeles we are too close to the factory to appreciate the tremendous influence the talking screen has upon the minds, imagination and thoughts of the people. Here we see the wheels going around; we rub elbows with the performers; we are constantly on location; the forest is obstructed by the trees. But even here the films are the biggest thing from a commercial as well as an entertainment standpoint.

A few months ago I took "a swing around the circle," visited thirty-two states and paid especial attention to the picture situation.

[1] See Editor's Note, Chapter XVI.

At that time the industry and the country at large was gravely concerned over the question of public morals in their relation to the films. The tendency, for several years, had been toward emphasis upon the sordid side of life—sex problems, gangster heroes, the exploitation of crime in its various phases and there was evidence that the public was fed up on this sort of fare. Movements were started within church organizations, effective boycotts alarmed producers. It seemed obvious that unless something radical was done a major disaster impended.

I talked with producers, some of whom were obsessed with the idea that no picture which was not shot through with double meanings, vulgar innuendo, sex, nakedness and smut could be a box-office success.

Will H. Hays, the so-called czar of the film industry, although no real czar would think of working the long hours Mr. Hays puts in or enduring the strain of what I came to believe was the busiest job in the country, did not agree. Neither could I believe that the people of the United States had fallen to such low estate. So I set out to take the pulse of 20,000,000 picture addicts.

It was a heartening experience. One that restored confidence in the integrity and basic soundness of the man on the street, who at frequent intervals became the man in the theatre chair.

I found many exhibitors with the same complex held by the producers. If a picture wasn't at least "broad," they said, the customers would stay away, but they were already staying away in impressive numbers and most of these theatre operators were willing to try an experiment in decency.

"Oh, that's all right for a church town like Philadelphia," I was told, "but New York or Boston or Chicago won't stand for the Pollyanna stuff."

Well, I went to New York and Boston and Chicago and fifty other towns, large, small, manufacturing, industrial, residential, prosperous, busted, disgusted or contented, and in not one single instance, once the veneer of self-conscious sophistication had been scratched away, did I find a hair breadth's variation on the part of the general public in a desire for films which held life up to a mirror and which reflected decency, courage, manliness and the finer things.

This is true in New York's Ghetto as on Buffalo's Delaware Avenue, or San Francisco's Nob Hill. Everywhere was the demand for pictures to which children could be taken without contamination or where a sister or mother could find amusement without embarrassment.

This investigator held no brief for the screen. I knew Will Hays as a high-minded executive fighting for a principle in which few others had any faith, but I also sensed that unless a complete about-face was made, Los Angeles would soon become known from Dan to Beersheba as the cesspool of the world and in that phase of the situation every business enterprise in Southern California was vitally interested.

Once convinced that every picture did not need to tell the story of a ruined lady or glorify a murderous thug, the industry set about putting its house in order with characteristic energy and ability and in less than a year a mighty change has come over the face of the picture makers.

The fear of Pollyanna so often given voice in my meetings with exhibitors and newspaper editors and publishers has gone, utterly routed in the face of such virile productions as "One Night of Love," "Gay Divorcee," "Roberta," "Flirtation Walk," "Naughty Marietta," "Unfinished Symphony," among the charming musical comedies. "It Happened One Night," "Broadway Bill," "The Little Colonel," "One More Spring," and similar films coming under the head of romantic comedy. "The White Parade," "Imitation of Life," "Clive of India," "Mighty Barnum," "House of Rothschild, ' Barretts of Wimpole Street," "Lives of a Bengal Lancer," in the heavier group, and so on through a long list of the finest examples of motion-picture art yet to find screen expression.

Schedules for this year are crowded with promises of just as good or better entertainment.

It has taken time to bring about this renaissance and the job is not finished. A considerable portion of the public is still skeptical; still looks askance at the Greeks bearing gifts, but business is constantly growing better and as a newspaper reporter, who was privileged to look behind many a drop and peer through peepholes in many a flat, I would like to retrace the trip I made constantly on the defensive, often apologetic.

I would like to go to Mr. Sinbad in Providence and Mr. Robinson in Knoxville, and Mr. Brown in New Orleans and look them straight in the eye and say: "You bet I'm from Los Angeles where the movies come from. We're proud of the pictures, of the producers and of the industry. They're the best gol-darned entertainment the world has ever known, and when better movies are made we're going to make them. I don't know the difference between a stand-in and a cut-back, but did you hear Charles Laughton recite Lincoln's Gettysburg Address in 'Ruggles of Red Gap' or see Fred Astaire and Ginger Rogers in 'Roberta?' Did you hear and see that little English boy bring David Copperfield back to life? No, by heck, there's nothing the matter with the movies, we'll tell the world."

As a matter of fact the pictures themselves must tell the world. They alone have the entree to every circle and make their appeal to every member of every family. No newspaper, magazine or broadcasting station can possibly have the widespread appeal of the motion picture. It carries its message in a universal language to the isles of the South Seas and the frozen North, from the golden shores of California to the rock-bound coast of Maine. It brings an hour of happiness to the distrait of Europe and for a modest coin harassed orientals obtain a glimpse of how the other half lives.

It was a great day for Southern California when motion pictures came into their own for, sooner or later, this permanent home of production will lose the scarlet letter pinned upon it through years of adjustment, and motion pictures will take their place as the greatest entertainment and educational factor within the purview of mankind.

"What does the picture mean to you?" I asked Mr. Hays the other day.

Here is his reply:

"One stands on a high mountain and sees long lines of men, women and children moving slowly forward. They come from everywhere. They are rosy-cheeked girls from the farms, and their paler-faced sisters from the cities whose feet ache from long hours of standing behind bargain counters. There are plow boys, and sons of millionaires, and boys with the sallow cheeks of the tenements. There are old women with hands reddened and coarsened by work, and with eyes grown listless with long waiting. There are old men who hobble on crooked sticks, and children with the flash of the sun's gold in their hair and the happy laughter of innocence in their voices. There are the schoolboy and the savant, and the man of no learning at all.

"There are men and women of every race and every tongue, moving slowly forward, seeking something, seeking, searching, yearning—asking for a place to dream. All about them is the roar of the cities, the confused, jangling noises of life that is hurried, rushed, propelled forward at a breathless speed. Every minute of every hour of every day they come—millions of them. And over and above them, and in front of them, attracting them on, offering that which they desire, are billions of flickering shadows—the motion picture. Who shall estimate its importance? Who shall attempt to say what it means to the world?"

ADDENDUM

WHO'S WHO AMONG THE CONTRIBUTORS

WILLIAM ALLEN WHITE is the Editor and owner of the *Emporia Daily* and *Weekly Gazette. Is the author of* "Stratagem and Spoils," "The Old Order Changeth," "Life of Woodrow Wilson," "Life of Calvin Coolidge," "Masks in a Pageant," and other literary works.

JOHN J. CANTWELL, D.D. The Most Reverend, is bishop of Los Angeles and San Diego.

EDWARD G. ROBINSON is one of America's foremost screen actors. Appeared in "Little Caesar," "The Silver Dollar," "The Whole Town's Talking," and many other screen successes. Prior to his coming to Hollywood, he was a member of the Theatre Guild Acting Company in New York and played leading parts in many of their productions.

RAYMOND J. CANNON is a member of Congress from Wisconsin and in 1934 introduced a bill for the National Censorship of Motion Pictures.

BEN B. LINDSEY is Judge of the Superior Court of Los Angeles, (elected 1934). For more than twenty-five years he was Judge of the Juvenile Court at Denver and is responsible for the establishment of similar courts throughout the United States. Is author of "The Revolt of Modern Youth," "Companionate Marriage," and other works.

BENJAMIN HORACE HIBBARD is Professor of Agricultural Economics at the University of Wisconsin; a member of American Farm Economic Association and American Academy of Politics and Science; author of "Effect of the Great War

252

on Agriculture," "The History of the Public Land Policies," etc.

JONAH J. GOLDSTEIN has been City Magistrate of the City of New York since 1931. Assisted in the drafting and passage of legislative reforms affecting the Family Court, Children's Court, and Magistrate's Court. Author of "The Family in Court," and "Social Service and the Law."

DON MARQUIS is a playwright and columnist. He is the author of "The Old Soak," "The Dark Hour," and other plays. Is a frequent contributor to America's best known magazines.

WILLIAM LYON PHELPS is Professor Emeritus of Yale University, writer and lecturer. Is critic and student of the Drama and author of "Twentieth Century Theatre," "Essays on Modern Dramatists," "Some Makers of American Literature," "Essays on Things," and others.

EDWIN SCHALLERT is dramatic critic of the *Los Angeles Times,* and owing to his proximity to Hollywood is one of our best informed commentators on the movies.

SEYMOUR STERN has had eight years' experience in motion-picture production in Hollywood. Author of screen-treatments and continuities. Contributor on motion pictures to New York *Times, New Republic, Modern Monthly, Close Up,* etc. Editor of *Experimental Cinema,* the only magazine in the United States devoted to the cinema as art.

GABRIELA MISTRAL (Lucille Godoy) is a native of Chile and the foremost poetess of South America. She is now the Chilean Consul at Madrid.

MARION A. ZEITLIN is instructor of Spanish at U. C. L. A.

BROCK PEMBERTON is one of Broadway's foremost producers. He introduced Pirandello to the United States with "Six Characters in Search of an Author." Among his better known productions are, "Enter Madame," "Lulu Bett," "Mister Pitt," and "Strictly Dishonorable." His current hit is "Personal Appearance."

WOLF W. MOSS hoboed through Europe, Africa and Asia and visited for information the theatres and movies in all countries. Was assistant director to Mr. Mamoulian at the Theatre Guild School for his production of "Enter Madame."

UPTON SINCLAIR is the author of "The Jungle," "King Coal," "Jimmy Higgins," "They Call Me Carpenter," "Boston," "The Wet Parade," and other books. He is the father of the Epic Plan. In 1934 he was the Democratic gubernatorial nominee in the State of California.

JOHN HAYNES HOLMES is the head of the Community Church in New York, which he organized after leaving the Unitarian ministry. He is editor of "Unity," (Chicago) and Associate editor of "The World Tomorrow." Author of "New Churches for Old," "Patriotism Is Not Enough," "A Sensible Man's View of Religion."

SIDNEY E. GOLDSTEIN is Associate Rabbi of the Free Synagogue, New York, Professor in Social Service, Jewish Institute of Religion, Chairman, Committee on Social Ethics, New York Board of Jewish Ministers, Chairman, Commission on Social Justice, Central Conference of American Rabbis, Author of "The Synagogue and Social Service," "The League of Nations and Grounds for Action in Behalf of Minority Groups," and other works in the field of social science and social action.

W. E. BLATZ is director of St. George's School for Child Study at the University of Toronto and a frequent contributor to the Child Training periodicals.

CHAPIN HALL is writer and journalist and correspondent for the Los Angeles Times.

WILLIAM J. PERLMAN is a playwright and ex-producer. Author of "My Country," "The Broken Chain," "The King Amuses Himself," and other plays. As co-producer of "Juno and the Paycock" he introduced Sean O'Casey to American audiences.